A PRAYER JOURNAL FOR EXPECTANT COUPLES

As We Grow Together:

A Prayer Journal for Expectant Couples

A PRAYER JOURNAL FOR EXPECTANT COUPLES

As We Grow Together:

A Prayer Journal for Expectant Couples

By

Rev. Onedia N. Gage, Ph.D.

A Prayer Journal for Expectant Couples

God's Words

God blessed them and said to them, "Be fruitful and increase in number; fill the earth and subdue it."

Genesis 1:28a

You will be with child and give birth to a son, and you are to give Him the name Jesus.

Luke 1:31

Blessed is she who has believed that what the Lord has said to her will be accomplished.

Luke 1:45

A PRAYER JOURNAL FOR EXPECTANT COUPLES

Dedication

To Hillary and Nehemiah

*For teaching me these lessons
And sharing your childhood wisdom with me.*

*I love you and hopefully your wisdom will come in
Handy for my grandchildren and great-grandchildren
and all future generations.*

To The New Parent

*You will grow from the life you will hold in your arms.
Be open and prayerful to what you will learn and
What you will experience.*

Give your children all of you—all of what you got!

AS WE GROW TOGETHER

Other Titles by
Reverend Onedia N. Gage, Ph.D.

Are You Ready for 9th Grade . . . Again? A Family's Guide to Success
As We Grow Together Daily Devotional for Expectant Couples
As We Grow Together Prayer Journal for Expectant Couples
As We Grow Together: Workbook for Expectant Couples Her Workbook
As We Grow Together: Workbook for Expectant Couples His Workbook
The Best 40 Days of Your Life: A Journey of Spiritual Renewal
The Blue Print: Poetry for the Soul
From Fat to Fit in 90 Days: A Fitness Journal
From Two to One: The Notebook for the Christian Couple
Hannah's Voice: Powerful Lessons in Prayer
Her Story: The Legacy of Her Fight The Devotional
Her Story: The Legacy of Her Fight The Legacy Journal
Her Story: The Legacy of Her Fight Prayers and Journal
ILY! A Mother Daughter Relationship Workbook
In Her Own Words: Notebook for the Christian Woman
In Purple Ink: Poetry for the Spirit
The Intensive Retreat for Couples for Her
The Intensive Retreat for Couples for Him
Living a Whole Life: Sermons which Promote, Prompt and Provoke Life
Love Letters to God from a Teenage Girl
The Measure of a Woman: The Details of Her Soul
The Notebook: For Me, About Me, By Me
The Notebook for the Christian Teen
On This Journey Daily Devotional for Young People
On This Journey Prayer Journal for Young People
On This Journey Prayer Journal for Young People, Volume 2
One Day More Than We Deserve Prayer Journal for the Growing Christian
Promises, Promises: A Christian Novel
Queen in the Making: Bible Study for Teen Girls
Six Months of Solitude: The Sanctity of Singleness Notebook
Tools for These Times: Timely Sermons for Uncertain Times
With An Anointed Voice: The Power of Prayer
Yielded and Submitted: A Woman's Journey for a Life Dedicated to God
Yielded and Submitted: A Woman's Journey for a Life Dedicated to God Intimate Study
Yielded and Submitted: A Woman's Journey for a Life Dedicated to God Prayers and Journal

A Prayer Journal for Expectant Couples

Library of Congress

As We Grow Together
A Prayer Journal for Expectant Couples

All Rights Reserved © 2009, 2017
Rev. Onedia N. Gage, Ph. D.

No part of this of book may be reproduced or transmitted in
Any form or by any means, graphic, electronic, or mechanical,
Including photocopying, recording, taping, or by any
Information storage or retrieval system, without the
Permission in writing from the publisher.

Purple Ink, Inc. Press

For Information address:
Purple Ink, Inc.
P O Box 300113
Houston, TX 77230
www.purpleink.net
onediagage@purpleink.net

Onedia Gage Ministries

www.onediagage.com
onediagage@onediagage.com

ISBN:
978-0-9801002-3-5

Printed in United States

As We Grow Together

Dear God,

Thank You for Your provision of this message. I have seen You do some most amazing things. I am certain that I did not deserve the opportunity to be the vessel for this amazing document. It has truly blessed my life and required me to reflect on how my time will never be the same.

I thank You for allowing me to bless others with my experiences and learnings. I will forever share the wisdom You gifted me with.

God, thank You for trusting me to share Your message and this work. I believe that I will be part of a great work and which I will never even know the full extent.

Thank You for gifting me with children. Thank You for letting me educate them, pray for them, love them, and be stewards of them. Please always keep them safe. I am concerned about their future, their health and their emotional well-being. I am just a vessel. You are their Keeper and Provider.

I am trying to stay focused on You so that I cannot get out of Your reach. Thank You again God for what You bless me with and how You continue to provide for me.

It is in Jesus' name I pray.

Amen.

Your Daughter,

Onedia

A Prayer Journal for Expectant Couples

AS WE GROW TOGETHER

To the Couple:

Thank you for selecting **As We Grow Together** as your prayer journal during your pregnancy. You are truly embarking on a blessing. Your pregnancy is a beautifully blessed time in your life. This special time in your life also needs to be a time of prayer, study, mediation, forgiveness and reflection.

The time passes more quickly than you realize. Pregnancy is also God's tool which He uses to teach us that nothing is forever and great things come to those who wait on the Lord. Pregnancy is also His message that He can do great things through us when we are submissive and obedient. And let His will be done in our lives. He has it all planned and timed out. He just needs our participation.

God sent His instruction to write this devotional and journal through a great friend. She called me on a Sunday to tell me she was pregnant. At the same time, I was pregnant and another great friend was pregnant, also. She told me that I should write this after I reminded her of <u>On This Journey: A Daily Devotional for Young People</u>. What she didn't know was that He had shown me the vision. She was the confirmation I needed to proceed.

In this devotional and journal series, you will investigate who you think you are and discover who will be as a new parent. For those of you thinking: "but I am not a new parent," I beg to differ. You are a new parent each time you parent. My mother was a different parent to me than she was to my sister. In between children, we grow, change, learn and decide to be different parents. So you will parent differently. Lastly, you are new to that little one and that little one is new to you. While experience is the best teacher, most of our experiences demand our change.

Enjoy this time. Use it wisely. Nothing can get time back. Enjoy all the intimate moments with your mate because this type of time together will not be the same again ever. Your child will change and impact the way you spend time together.

May these words bless your pregnancy and the relationship between the two of you. In this journal, I will often suggest you two are married, because you are. For the duration of the life of the child, you will intersect and be reminded of one another. So if you are not married and don't intend to be, proceed with caution. By the end, you may want to be married, maybe not to him or her, but to someone.

A Prayer Journal for Expectant Couples

God Bless You,

Onedia N. Gage

Onedia N. Gage

How to Use this Prayer Journal

Dear New Parent:

Just a few suggestions:

- Mark your Bible with the scriptures that we study in the devotional. You may need them later in your life.

- Feel free to go as you need based on topics.

- Read the devotional daily. It is helpful for the two of you to both read the devotional. This will serve as discussion topics for you.

- Pray with your spouse.

- Pray for your spouse.

- Pray for your unborn child.

- Pray for yourself.

- Journal your pregnancy.

- Enjoy your time together.

A PRAYER JOURNAL FOR EXPECTANT COUPLES

TABLE OF CONTENTS

Scriptures
Dedication
Letter to Expectant Couple
Instructions for Use

Week One:	Chosen
Week Two:	Love & Intimacy with Your Spouse
Week Three:	Your Role as Woman and Wife
Week Four:	Your Role as Man and Husband
Week Five:	Your Role as Mother
Week Six:	Your Role as Father
Week Seven:	Your Role as Parents
Week Eight:	Your Parents
Week Nine:	Communication with Your Spouse
Week Ten:	Your Communication with God
Week Eleven:	Pray for Yourself and Your Spouse
Week Twelve:	Prayer as a Parent
Week Thirteen:	Prayers for Your Children
Week Fourteen:	Vision: A Game Plan with God's Leadership
Week Fifteen:	Vision: A Financial Strategy
Week Sixteen:	Love: God's Definition
Week Seventeen:	Love: God Exhibits His Love
Week Eighteen:	Loving Your Spouse
Week Nineteen:	Loving Your Spouse
Week Twenty:	Love Yourself
Week Twenty-One:	Love Yourself: The Fruit of the Spirit
Week Twenty-Two:	Love Yourself: The Fruit of the Spirit, Part 2
Week Twenty-Three:	Taking Care of Yourself: An Act of Love
Week Twenty-Four:	Parent As A Teacher
Week Twenty-Five:	Lifestyle Changes
Week Twenty-Six:	Parenthood Has Its Rewards
Week Twenty-Seven:	Faith is Required for Parents
Week Twenty-Eight:	The Lessons Ahead
Week Twenty-Nine:	Life is Short — Do What Matters
Week Thirty:	In Ten Weeks
Week Thirty-One:	Birth and Its Complexities
Week Thirty-Two:	Biblical Parents
Week Thirty-Three:	Biblical Parents
Week Thirty-Four:	Complex Family Discrepancies
Week Thirty-Five:	Children of the Bible
Week Thirty-Six:	Parenting Great Children
Week Thirty-Seven:	What Kind of Parent Would Jesus Be?

A Prayer Journal for Expectant Couples

Week Thirty-Eight: Parenting Effectively
Week Thirty-Nine: Enjoy Each Other
Week Forty: Seven Days of Prayer

Afterword
Acknowledgements
About the Author

The Prayer Journal

A PRAYER JOURNAL FOR EXPECTANT COUPLES

Week One
Chosen

Congratulations and blessings! God chose you and your spouse to carry and birth His child. How exciting?! Pregnancy is an awesome time for you and your spouse. I am going to do my best not to simply address this as a woman's devotional. The pregnancy deserves the equal investment of both of you.

Parents are chosen. Count it as the blessing it is and with the reverence it deserves. There are many women who want to be pregnant and can't. This inability plagues them, causes the end of all possibilities to be reached and most options exhausted, including increased emotional anxiety and decreased financial means. There is no explanation needed to explain either event, because both events involve blessings, whether seen or not.

God chose you and your spouse for a time such as this, so we will discuss and discover some of the best uses of this time.

Be reminded – His plans, thoughts and ways are not ours. So now that we have accepted God's plan – our pregnancy – move forward to uncover the other treasures which accompany this awesome journey of this miracle.

Sunday	He chose you and your spouse to bear a child/children. John 15:16; Luke 1:30; Matthew 22:14
Monday	Children are gifts from God Luke 1:42 (Luke 1)
Tuesday	You and your spouse are made for each other. Genesis 2:22-24; Matthew 19:6
Wednesday	He designed you for a time such as this. Ecclesiastes 3:1, 2a
Thursday	When God is doing His will, expect some storms. Matthew 1:20-21
Friday & Saturday	Expect and prepare for His good and perfect will

A Prayer Journal for Expectant Couples
1 John 5:14-15; 1 Thessalonians 5:18;
Revelation 4:11

AS WE GROW TOGETHER

Week One – Sunday
He Chose You and Your Spouse To Bear a Child/Children
Matthew 22:14; Luke 1:30; John 15:16

[14]Many are invited, but few are chosen.

Matthew 22:14

_____
_____
_____
_____
_____
_____
_____
_____
_____
_____
_____
_____
_____
_____
_____
_____
_____
_____
_____
_____
_____

A Prayer Journal for Expectant Couples

Week One – Monday
Children Are Gifts From God
Luke 1

[42]In a loud voice she exclaimed: "Blessed are you among women, and blessed is the child you will bear"!

Luke 1:42

_____
_____
_____
_____
_____
_____
_____
_____
_____
_____
_____
_____
_____
_____
_____
_____
_____
_____
_____
_____
_____
_____
_____
_____

As We Grow Together

Week One – Tuesday
You and Your Spouse Are Made For Each Other
Genesis 2:22-24; Matthew 19:5-6

[22] Then the Lord God made a woman from the rib He had taken out of the man, and he brought her to the man. [23] The man said, "This is now bone of my bones and flesh of my flesh; she shall be called 'woman,' for she was taken out of man." [24] For this reason a man will leave his father and mother and be united to his wife, and they will become one flesh.

Genesis 2:22-24

[6b] "Therefore what God has joined together, let no man separate."

Matthew 19:6

_____
_____
_____
_____
_____
_____
_____
_____
_____
_____
_____
_____
_____
_____
_____
_____
_____
_____
_____
_____

A Prayer Journal for Expectant Couples

Week One – Wednesday
He Designed You for a Time Such As This
Ecclesiastes 3:1-2a

[1]There is a time for everything, and a season for every activity under heaven: [2] a time to be born

Ecclesiastes 3:1-2a

AS WE GROW TOGETHER

Week One – Thursday
When God is Doing His Will, Expect Some Storms

[20]But after he had considered this, an angel of the Lord appeared to him in a dream and said, "Joseph son of David, do not be afraid to take Mary as your wife, because what is conceived in her is from the Holy Spirit. [21]She will give birth to a son, and you are to give him the name Jesus, because He will save His people from their sins.
Matthew 1:20-21

A Prayer Journal for Expectant Couples

Week One – Friday
Expect and Prepare for God's Good and Perfect Will
Revelation 4:11; 1 John 5:14-15; 1 Thessalonians 5:18

[14]This is the confidence we have in approaching God: that if we ask anything according to His will, He hears us. [15]And if we know that He hears us—whatever we ask—we know that we have what we asked of Him.

1 John 5:14-15

AS WE GROW TOGETHER

Week One – Saturday
Expect and Prepare for God's Good and Perfect Will
Revelation 4:11; 1 John 5:14-15; 1 Thessalonians 5:18
Part 2

[11] "You are worthy, our Lord and God, to receive glory and honor and power, for You created all things, and by Your will they were created and have their being."

Revelation 4:11

[18] give thanks in all circumstances, for this is God's will for you in Christ Jesus.

1 Thessalonians 5:18

Week Two
Love & Intimacy with Your Spouse

Your relationship with your mate is extremely important. This relationship stimulates the life of your child. This relationship is the basis of how the child is raised. If a child sees love and feels loved, then she will love. Children are excellent imitators of their environments.

Love and intimacy with your spouse needs nurturing and cultivating. It deserves your attention. Love and intimacy should be kept as a high level. You each need this love and intimacy. Love and intimacy fuels your marriage. You will need this energy.

One such tool is <u>The Five Love Languages</u> by Dr. Gary Chapman. Dr. Chapman provides tools and equipment for the renewal, revival and resurgence of love in your marriage. He offers solutions for longtime marital problems and stumbling blocks. I promise you that a great, loving, and intimate relationship makes it easier to make the sacrifices for this baby.

Over the next seven days we will do a review of Dr. Gary Chapman's book with biblical applications for your marriage and your child.

I encourage you to read <u>The Five Love Languages</u> and <u>The Five Love Languages for Children</u> by Dr. Gary Chapman.

AS WE GROW TOGETHER

Week Two — Sunday
Love & Intimacy With Your Spouse
Song of Solomon 2:10a; 3:4

[10a] My lover is mine and I am his.

Song of Solomon 2:10a

A Prayer Journal for Expectant Couples

Week Two — Monday
Words of Affirmation

Dr. Chapman also recommends notes and letters to affirm your mate. He also suggests your personally post yourself a reminder of how important words are. If your language is words, then you should share how your mate can fill your love tank with words.

As We Grow Together

Week Two — Tuesday
Quality Time

Quality time is the second of the love languages. Dr. Gary Chapman describes fluidly the importance of quality time. This happens to be my love language. One evening during my pregnancy we were out to dinner. A couple spoke to us saying enjoy each moment, each meal at its intended temperature, each late morning and early night.

A Prayer Journal for Expectant Couples

Week Two — Wednesday
Receiving Gifts

Everyone (almost) likes receiving gifts. Some people, however, need gifts to know they are loved. Spontaneous or planned; simple or extravagant; big or small – it doesn't matter. This love language is not to be misunderstood or confused with buying your mate's affections or love. The gift is an expression the other person's thoughts and demonstrates how much they care.

AS WE GROW TOGETHER

Week Two — Thursday
Acts of Service

How does your wife make you feel when she does something for you because you needed help? How does it feel when your husband remembers your requests? If your response is loved, cared for, remembered, or excited, then this is your love language. What people do for you, especially your mate, is more important than anything else that can happen to you.

A Prayer Journal for Expectant Couples

Week Two — Friday
Physical Touch

Physical touch during your pregnancy and during your delivery becomes invaluable. Physical touch includes hugs, touches, kisses, massages, and sexual intercourse. Physical touch needs to be a priority in your relationship. You have to be honest with your mate about your needs and what your desires are. Be open to respond to meet those needs.

AS WE GROW TOGETHER

Week Two — Saturday
Keep Your Love Tank Full

Your love tank is where your emotional wellness is measured. Dr. Chapman states that keeping the love tank full (p. 23) is essential to your marriage. A full love tank will enhance the health of your marriage. Everyone desires a healthy marriage. A full love tank ensures a healthy and fulfilling marriage.

A PRAYER JOURNAL FOR EXPECTANT COUPLES

Week Three

Your Role as Woman and Wife

God has a job description for us. He clearly defines our role and duties as a woman and a wife. God is quite orderly and He was certain that the woman has a place. He was certain that the wife has a role and duties. Over the next seven days, we will examine our role and responsibilities. For some this will be new – for others a simple refresher or reminder. In either case, our marriages and lives will progress much smoother if we learn to function within our roles. We don't have a problem with knowing, but we have trouble within the parameters of our role. What do I mean? God designed life to follow certain criteria and guidelines. When we choose to divert from those then we create conflict and confusion. I think that we are God's best creation, and we should act as such.

There are times when it is hard to be a great wife. There are times when it's harder than others to be wise and supportive. But then there are times when it is an awesome experience to be a woman and a wife. You will experience a love of that son.

Motherhood moves you to reexamine your first roles and responsibilities more carefully. These roles and responsibilities need to be active and functioning as you prepare for your baby. We will investigate the roles, responsibilities, and action plans for achieving success in these.

Sunday	God made woman as a helper to man Genesis 2:20b-25
Monday	(Womanhood defined) A Noble Wife is a Noble Woman First 1 Kings 3:12; Ephesians 4:22-24; 4:32; 5:40; 6:18
Tuesday	The Wife of Noble Character, Part 1 Proverbs 31:10-17
Wednesday	The Wife of Noble Character, Part 2 Proverbs 31:18-31
Thursday	Your Role as Wife Ephesians 5:22-33

Friday	Wives and Our Higher Calling 1 Peter 3:1-7
Saturday	Wives, Some Final Instructions Colossians 3:18; 4:2, 6

Week Three — Sunday
God Made Eve as a Helper
Genesis 2:20b-25

[20b] But for Adam no suitable helper was found. [22] Then the Lord God made a woman from the rib He had taken out of the man, and He brought her to the man.

Genesis 2:20b, 22

As We Grow Together

Week Three — Monday
A Noble Wife is a Noble Woman First:
Womanhood Defined
Ephesians 4:22-24; 4:32; 5:10; 6:18; 1 Kings 3:12

[10b] and find out what pleases the Lord.

Ephesians 5:10b

A Prayer Journal for Expectant Couples

Week Three — Tuesday
The Wife of Noble Character – Part 1
Proverbs 31:10-17

[10] A wife of noble character who can find? She is worth far more than rubies.

Proverbs 31:10

As We Grow Together

Week Three — Wednesday
The Wife of Noble Character – Part 2
Proverbs 31:18-31

[29] "Many women do noble things, but you surpass them all."

Proverbs 31:29

A Prayer Journal for Expectant Couples

Week Three — Thursday
Your Role as Wife
Ephesians 5:22-23

^{22}Wives, submit to your husbands as to the Lord. ^{33b}and the wife must respect her husband.

Ephesians 5:22, 33b

As We Grow Together

Week Three — Friday
Wives and Our Higher Calling
1 Peter 3:1-7

⁴Instead, it should be that of your inner self, the unfading beauty of a gentle and quiet spirit, which is of great worth in God's sight.

1 Peter 3:4

A Prayer Journal for Expectant Couples

Week Three — Saturday
Wives, Some Final Instructions
Colossians 3:18; 4:2, 6

[18]Wives, submit to your husbands, as is fitting in the Lord.
[2]Devote yourselves to prayer, being watchful and thankful.
[6]Let your conversation be always full of grace, seasoned with salt, so that you may know how to answer everyone.

Colossians 3:18; 4:2, 6

Week Four
Your Role as Man and Husband

God has a job description for men. He clearly defines your role as a man and the duties of a man, husband, and father. God is quite orderly and He was certain that the man has a place. A significant place: man has a job and is the head of the woman and his home. God's first order of business was to give Adam a job.

Over the next seven days we will examine Adam's job, role, and responsibilities. The Bible clearly articulates God's stance on all matters regarding man and His expectations of man.

Men, and women, too, for that matter, this is a call to action. Man, your role is as difficult as it is rewarding; is as challenging as it is awesome; is as complex as it is delicate; is as confusing as it is honorable. Men, to whom much is given, much is required.

Men, your role is important and extremely valuable. Over the next week, we will uncover tools for your role and responsibilities. We will provide resources for encouragement during your journey as a man and husband. Value exists in your success in your role. Successfully functioning in your role is critical to the growth and advancement of the family. So, we will also provide tools and resources for family success.

You have a hard job, but the rewards are great. Enjoy the journey.

Sunday	God creates man in His own image; Man defined Genesis 1:26-27; 2:7
Monday	God employs man; Man's role Genesis 1:28-30; 2:19-25
Tuesday	"(Adam), Where Are You"? Genesis 3:9, 12, 17a
Wednesday	He who findeth a wife findeth a **good** thing. But who are you? Proverbs 18:22 KJV
Thursday	Love your wife; Your role as a husband Ephesians 5:22-23; Colossians 3:19

A Prayer Journal for Expectant Couples

Friday   Loving Your Wife, Part 2
                  Ephesians 5:22-23; Colossians 3:19

Saturday   The "Honey-Do" List
                  1 Peter 3:1-7

AS WE GROW TOGETHER

Week Four — Sunday
God Creates Man in His Own Image; Man defined
Genesis 1:26, 27; 2:7

[26]Then God said, "Let us make man in our image, in our likeness, and let them rule over the fish of the sea and the birds of the air, over the livestock, over all the earth and over all the creatures that move along the ground.

Genesis 1:26

A Prayer Journal for Expectant Couples

Week Four — Monday
God Employs Man
Genesis 1:28-30; 2:19-25

[28] God blessed them and said to them, "Be fruitful and increase in number; fill the earth and subdue it. Rule over the fish of the sea and the birds of the air and over every living creature that moves on the ground."

Genesis 1:28

As We Grow Together

Week Four — Tuesday
Adam, Where Are You?
Genesis 3:9-12, 17a

[11] And He said, "Who told you that you were naked? Have you eaten from the tree that I commanded you not to eat from"?

Genesis 3:11

A Prayer Journal for Expectant Couples

Week Four — Wednesday
But Who Are You?
Proverbs 18:22 (KJV)

[22] He who findeth a wife, findeth a good thing.

Proverbs 18:22 (KJV)

As We Grow Together

Week Four — Thursday
Your Role as a Husband: Loving Your Wife
Ephesians 5:22-33; Colossians 3:19

[25]Husbands, love your wives, first as Christ loved the church and gave himself up for her. [28b]He who loves his wife as he loves himself. [19]Husbands, love your wives and do not be hard with them.

Ephesians 5:25, 28b; Colossians 3:19

A Prayer Journal for Expectant Couples

Week Four — Friday
Loving Your Wife, Part 2
Ephesians 5:22-23; Colossians 3:19

[28b]He who loves his wife as he loves himself.

Ephesians 5:28b

As We Grow Together

Week Four — Saturday
The "Honey-Do" List
1 Peter 3:1-7

⁷Husbands, in the same way be considerate as you live with your wives, and treat them with respect as the weaker partner and as heirs with you of the gracious gift of life, so that nothing hinders your prayers.

1 Peter 3:7

_____
_____
_____
_____
_____
_____
_____
_____
_____
_____
_____
_____
_____
_____
_____
_____
_____
_____
_____
_____
_____
_____
_____
_____

Week Five
Your Role as Mother

Motherhood is an awesome gift. Your life will never be the same and it is no longer your own. Motherhood is also a tremendous gift and responsibility. Nothing is quite so rewarding as motherhood – not even fatherhood can measure up.

I certainly desired a child, but I didn't know I was ready. When I conceived, I was scared because I didn't know if I could do a great job. I had no idea how to do a great job. I had a few good examples, but could I be a mother, ultimately the mother God expected me to be?

In the next seven days, I give my seven stars of motherhood. These are my observations on the foundations of a great motherhood – the tools I've used so far. By the way, most plans you make may not materialize. Don't fear, though, the baby will have clothes to wear home and your husband can go home for the car seat, and without the epidural you planned, the baby will still come and you will still be sane when it's over.

Your role is broad, yet vague; rewarding, yet difficult; inspiring, yet revealing; powerful and life-altering. I do know this in her first 18 months, I have learned more than all of my life. She teaches me something new daily and surprises me daily, as well.

Motherhood is a journey, rather than destination. My last points are (1) maintain your sense of humor; (2) call your mother or mother-figure daily, and (3) your only real job is to feed her. No matter what happens, Hillary eats, is warm, has clothes and shoes, and I hold her and hug her so that she feels my love in her language.

Sunday		Your Self-Portrait: What Do You See? Psalms 139:14
Monday		A Godly Woman Proverbs 31:28
Tuesday		In the Spirit Galatians 5:22-23
Wednesday		Wisdom at Work Proverbs 3:5-6; 31:26
Thursday		Teaching God's Word

AS WE GROW TOGETHER

                      Matthew 28:20

Friday   Powerful Relationship Builders (so a man thinketh)
                      Exodus 20:12; Matthew 5:5; Ephesians 13:19-20

Saturday   The Reap/Sow Principle
                      2 Corinthians 9:6

A Prayer Journal for Expectant Couples

Week Five — Sunday
Your Self-Portrait: What do you see?
Psalms 139:14; Isaiah 55:8

[14]I praise you because I am fearfully and wonderfully made; [8]"For my thought are not your thoughts and my ways are not your ways," declares the Lord.

Psalms 139:14; Isaiah 55:8

_____

_____

_____

_____

_____

_____

_____

_____

_____

_____

_____

_____

_____

_____

_____

_____

_____

_____

_____

_____

_____

_____

_____

_____

As We Grow Together

Week Five — Monday
A Godly Woman
Proverbs 31:28

[28] Her children arise and call her blessed; her husband also, and he praises her.

Proverbs 31:28

A Prayer Journal for Expectant Couples

Week Five — Tuesday
In The Spirit
Galatians 5:22-23 (KJV)

[22]But the fruit of the Spirit is love, joy, peace, long suffering gentleness, goodness, faith, [23]meekness, temperance; against such things there is no law.

Galatians 5:22-23 (KJV)

AS WE GROW TOGETHER

Week Five — Wednesday
Wisdom At Work
Proverbs 3:5-6; 31:26

⁵Trust in the Lord with all your heart and lean not on your own understanding; ⁶In all your ways acknowledge Him and He will direct your path. ²⁶She speaks with wisdom, and faithful instruction is on her tongue.

Proverbs 3:5-6; 31:26

Week Five — Thursday
Teaching God's Word
Matthew 28:20

[20]"and teaching them to obey everything I have commanded you. And surely I am with you always, to the very end of the age."

Matthew 28:20

AS WE GROW TOGETHER

Week Five — Friday
Powerful Relationship Builders
Exodus 20:12; Matthew 5:5; Ephesians 3:19-20

[12]Honor your father and your mother, so that you may live long in the land the Lord your God is giving you. [5]Blessed are the meek for they shall inherit the earth. [19]and to know this love that surpasses knowledge – that you may be filled to the measure of all the fullness of God. [20]Now to Him who is able to do immeasurably more than all we ask or imagine, according to His power at work on us.

Exodus 20:12; Matthew 5:5; Ephesians 3:19-20

A Prayer Journal for Expectant Couples

Week Five — Saturday
The Reap/Sow Principle
2 Corinthians 9:6

⁶Remember this: Whoever sows sparingly will also reap sparingly, and whoever sows generously will also reap generously.

2 Corinthians 9:6

Week Six
Your Role as Father

Dad. Father. Daddy. Pop-Pa. Whatever your child calls you, you are responsible for their growth, for their love tanks; for their knowledge and their behavior. Girls love you. Boys reverence you. They grow to understand you as their role model and example for their lives and leadership.

Being a dad has changed since you were a child. Your role at home will be different from that of your dad. Your dad may have never done the laundry or change a diaper, but you will probably do the laundry, change a diaper or whatever your family needs of you to support the family. You need to evaluate what your family needs and fill that need. These needs will be new for you to fill but valuable to your family.

Further, you need to ask your wife what her expectations are. Actively listening to her and taking notice of her expectations and needs will certainly insure the growth and success of your family. When your wife shares that she needs your help, ask what that means. Each wife will define help differently. Your wife may define help as prayer daily, studying daily and weekly, talking to her as needed, taking responsibility for taking the baby to and from daycare, among other things. Initially, your increased responsibilities seemed like a lot of work for you. With all that you are responsible for, you may wonder what she is doing. So ask her. When she shares what she does, don't be surprised; you will soon realize that you still do less but your role is equally as important and it benefits her and the family. Knowing that should make you understand the importance of your role and duties.

Fathers, your family needs your undivided attention. They also need your investment.

Dads, you are important to the total success. BE PRESENT.

Sunday	Your wisdom counts James 1:5; Proverbs 3:1-2, 7
Monday	Actions Speak Louder than Words Deuteronomy 9:18; 1 Corinthians 13:11; Ephesians 4:31; Proverbs 31:28
Tuesday	Actions Speak Louder than Words, Pt. 2 1 Samuel 13:14; 16:7; Psalm 51:10; Proverbs 27:19

A Prayer Journal for Expectant Couples

Wednesday	Disciplinarian Proverbs 3:11-12; 13:24
Thursday	Provocation Ephesians 6:14; Colossians 3:21
Friday	Patience (Anger) Ephesians 4:2-3
Saturday	Love Ephesians 5:1-2

AS WE GROW TOGETHER

Week Six — Sunday
Your Wisdom Counts
James 1:5; Proverbs 3:1-2, 7

[5]If any of you lacks wisdom, he should ask God, who gives generously to all without finding fault, and it will be given to him.
[1]My son, do not forget my teaching, but keep my commands in your heart, [2]for they will prolong your life for many years and bring you prosperity. [7]Do not be wise in your own eyes, fear the Lord and shun evil.

James 1:5; Proverbs 3:1-2, 7

A Prayer Journal for Expectant Couples
Week Six — Monday
Actions Speak Louder Than Words
Deuteronomy 9:18; 1 Corinthians 13:11; Ephesians 4:31; Proverbs 31:28

[18]Then once again I fell prostrate before the Lord for forty days and forty nights; I ate no bread and drank no water because of all the sin you had committed, doing what was evil in the Lord's sight and so provoking him to anger. "When I was a child, I talked like a child, I thought like a child, I reasoned like a child. When I became a man, I put childish ways behind me.
[31]Get rid of all bitterness, rage and anger, brawling and slander, along with every form of malice.
[28]Her children arise and call her blessed; her husband also, and he praises her.

Deuteronomy 9:18; 1 Corinthians 13:11; Ephesians 4:31; Proverbs 31:28

As We Grow Together

Week Six — Tuesday
Actions Speak Louder Than Words, Pt. 2
1 Samuel 13:14; 16:7; Psalm 51:10; Proverbs 27:19

[14] But now your kingdom will not endure; the Lord has sought out a man after his own heart and appointed him leader of his people, because you have not kept the Lord's command.

[7b] The Lord does not look at the things man looks at. Man looks at the outward appearance, but the Lord looks at the heart."

[10] Create in me a pure heart, O God, and renew a steadfast spirit within me.

[19] As water reflects a fact, so a man's heart reflects a man.

1 Samuel 13:14; 16:7; Psalm 51:10; Proverbs 27:19

A Prayer Journal for Expectant Couples

Week Six — Wednesday
Disciplinarian
Proverbs 3:11-12; 13:24

[11]My son, do not despise the Lord's discipline and do not resent his rebuke, [12]because the Lord disciplines those he loves, as a father the son he delights in. [24]He who spares the rod hates his son, but he who loves him is careful to discipline him.

Proverbs 3:11-12; 13:24

As We Grow Together

Week Six — Thursday
Provocation
Ephesians 6:4; Colossians 3:21

⁴Fathers, do not exasperate your children; instead, bring them up in the training and instruction of the Lord.
²¹Fathers, do not embitter your children, or they will become discouraged.

Ephesians 6:4; Colossians 3:21

_____
_____
_____
_____
_____
_____
_____
_____
_____
_____
_____
_____
_____
_____
_____
_____
_____
_____
_____
_____
_____
_____
_____
_____

A Prayer Journal for Expectant Couples
Week Six — Friday
Patience/Anger
Ephesians 4:2-3

²Be completely humble and gentle; be patient, bearing with one another in love. ³Make every effort to keep the unity of the Spirit through the bond of peace.

Ephesians 4:2-3

Week Six — Saturday
Love
Ephesians 5:1-2

¹Be imitators of God, therefore, as dearly loved children ²and live a life of love, just as Christ loved us and gave himself up for us as a fragrant offering and sacrifice to God.

Ephesians 5:1-2

A Prayer Journal for Expectant Couples

Week Seven
Your Role as Parents

Proverbs 4 discusses wisdom at length. God expects parents to gain wisdom and information through experience and reading. God also expects us to pray for wisdom.

God clearly explains our role and fully expects that we will carry out that role completely to His specifications. Parenthood is a gift and should not be treated as a burden. As parents, we are to offer God-given instruction to our children and lead by example. Use this time to clearly define your expectations of yourselves. Many times we have said, "I will never do . . ." or "I will always do . . ." Those statements, while at the time genuine, are poorly timed for first-time parents. First-time parents lack the necessary experience to anticipate the reality of the situations which will arise.

Use this time to unite intimately with God and one another. Let, allow, permit, and surrender to God to cover your anxiety, meet all your needs and cover your fears. God had a pre-developed plan; allow Him to show you His plan and use you to bring His well-developed plan to fruition.

Parents have very specific instructions from God. Parenting is not easy. We are stewards over the child and we are accountable to God for their lives. Parenthood is an awesome responsibility. Parenthood surpasses all other lifetime milestones. Parenthood should be cherished and for the gift that it is. Use this time to make a commitment to your God-given role.

Sunday	Parenting and Our Christian Lives Ephesians 4:17-32
Monday	Our Timing Ecclesiastes 3:1-8
Tuesday	Faithfulness Hebrews 11
Wednesday	Marriage – Honorable Hebrews 13:4
Thursday	God's Blessed Assurance Hebrews 13:5

Friday	Peaceful Parenting 1 Corinthians 7:15; 14:33
Saturday	Peaceful Parents Philippians 4:7

A Prayer Journal for Expectant Couples

Week Seven — Sunday
Parenting and Our Christian Lives
Ephesians 4:17-32

[32]Be kind and compassionate to one another, forgiving each other, just as in Christ God forgave you.

Ephesians 4:32

_____
_____
_____
_____
_____
_____
_____
_____
_____
_____
_____
_____
_____
_____
_____
_____
_____
_____
_____
_____
_____
_____
_____
_____
_____
_____
_____

As We Grow Together

Week Seven — Monday
Our Timing
Ecclesiastes 3:1-8

¹There is a time for everything, and a season for every activity under heaven.

Ecclesiastes 3:1

A Prayer Journal for Expectant Couples

Week Seven — Tuesday
Faithfulness is Crucial
Hebrews 11

[1]Now faith is being sure of what we hope for and certain of what we do not see.

Hebrews 11:1

AS WE GROW TOGETHER

Week Seven — Wednesday
Marriage – Honorable
Hebrews 13:4

[4]Marriage should be honored by all, and the marriage bed kept pure, for God will judge the adulterer and all the sexually immoral.

Hebrews 13:4

_____
_____
_____
_____
_____
_____
_____
_____
_____
_____
_____
_____
_____
_____
_____
_____
_____
_____
_____
_____
_____
_____
_____
_____

A Prayer Journal for Expectant Couples

Week Seven — Thursday
God's Blessed Assurance
Hebrews 13:5

⁵Keep your lives free from the love of money and be content with what you have, because God has said, "Never will I leave you; never will I forsake you."

Hebrew 13:5

Week Seven — Friday
Peaceful Parenting
1 Corinthians 7:15; 14:33

[15b]God has called us to live in peace. [33]For god is not a God of disorder but of peace.

1 Corinthians 7:15; 14:33

A Prayer Journal for Expectant Couples

Week Seven — Saturday
Peaceful Parents
Philippians 4:7

[7] And the peace of God, which transcends all understanding, will guard your hearts and your minds in Christ Jesus.

Philippians 4:7

Week Eight
Your Parents

Your example of relationship is critical for your success as a parent. Your relationship with your parents dictates your own relationship with your child as a parent. Are we doomed? Certainly not. Quite the contrary. You define your relationship based on what you experienced. You have a chance to change what happened as a parent based on what you experienced from your parents.

Now the important piece of your relationship with the parents is your own behavior. Your behavior has to be focused on God's word – not what your parents did or didn't do. I know initially this will be hard for some of us. However, don't despair, you too can forgive them and overcome your issues, as well as change your behavior to inspire a change in them. At the least, you will be able to reconcile yourself so you are able to parent without hindrance.

Be ever reminded we will be different parents from our parents and our parents' parents. We have extremely different resources and equally different responsibilities from our parents. Also, for me I have different parental goals and desires. As a new parent, we have a chance to develop our parental wish list – the ideas and decisions we will execute as parents, which are not subject to anyone's approval but God's. My priority is communication. Historically, parents don't talk about issues or share family historical information. Most of this information would be instrumental in making better decisions as teens and adults. I want our children as prepared as possible for as many health and financial issues as possible. Those are two areas where I personally struggle.

Sunday	Honor Your Parents Exodus 20:12
Monday	Cursed Deuteronomy 27:16
Tuesday	Death Leviticus 20:9
Wednesday	Forgiveness Matthew 6:14-15; 18:22

A Prayer Journal for Expectant Couples

Thursday   Sow & Reap
                Galatians 6:7

Friday   Leave & Cleave
                Genesis 2:24

Saturday   Follow Instructions
                Proverbs 1:8

Week Eight — Sunday
Honor Your Parents
Exodus 20:12

¹²Honor your father and your mother, so that you may live long in the land the Lord your God is giving you.

Exodus 20:12

A Prayer Journal for Expectant Couples

Week Eight — Monday
Cursed
Deuteronomy 27:16

[16]"Cursed is the man who dishonors his father or his mother."

Deuteronomy 27:16

AS WE GROW TOGETHER

Week Eight — Tuesday
Death
Leviticus 20:9

⁹If anyone curses his father or mother, he must be put to death. He has cursed his father or his mother, and his blood will be on his own head.

Leviticus 20:9

A Prayer Journal for Expectant Couples

Week Eight — Wednesday
Forgiveness
Matthew 6:14-15; 18:22

[14]For if you forgive men when they sin against you, your heavenly Father will also forgive you. [15]But if you do not forgive men their sins, your Father will not forgive your sins. [22]Jesus answered, "I tell you, not seven times, but seventy-seven times."

Matthew 6:14-15; 18:22

AS WE GROW TOGETHER

Week Eight — Thursday
Sow & Reap
Galatians 6:7

[7]Do not be deceived: God cannot be mocked. A man reaps what he sows.

Galatians 6:7

A Prayer Journal for Expectant Couples

Week Eight — Friday
Leave and Cleave
Genesis 2:24

[24]For this reason a man will leave his father and mother and be united to his wife, and they will become one flesh.

Genesis 2:24

As We Grow Together

Week Eight — Saturday
Follow Instructions
Proverbs 1:8

⁸Listen, my son, to your father's instruction and do not forsake your mother's teaching.

Proverbs 1:8

A Prayer Journal for Expectant Couples

Week Nine
Communication With Your Spouse

Did you marry your spouse because you loved to talk to them? Do you still love talking to your spouse? Do you talk about the same topics? Do you talk the same length of time to your spouse? Do you look into your spouse's eyes for the deep intimacy you did when you were courting?

Quality communication with your spouse is essential and crucial to a quality marriage and quality parenting. Quality communication requires your attention to details and your consistency, your truth, your memory, your active listening and your unconditional love.

Most times when communication lacks in your marriage, you and your spouse need to investigate the root of the problem. There may be any number of causes but the communication needs to be corrected immediately. Now some couples may never have communication issues. This is definitely a blessing. But for those of us who do or have had these problems we will address how to handle those possible issues this week.

Great communication is the cornerstone of the essential components of a great marriage. Communication requires work on both parties and commitment to success of both parties. Will we be working and committed on the same level at the same time at all times? Well no, but what we are trying to achieve is the working commitment for the goals of a great marriage and great communication:

Sunday	How do you settle disagreements? Ephesians 4:26-27
Monday	Your Spouse's Love Language Ephesians 5:22-33
Tuesday	Your Family's Mission Statement Isaiah 32:8
Wednesday	The plan for the child's care Proverbs 20:18a
Thursday	Are we on the same page? 2 Corinthians 13:11b, c

AS WE GROW TOGETHER

Friday	You and Your Spouse's Communication: What, When & Where? Ephesians 4:32, 1 Peter 3:8-9
Saturday	You and Your Spouse Communicate: How and Why? Ephesians 4:32, 1 Peter 3:8-9

A Prayer Journal for Expectant Couples

Week Nine — Sunday
How Do You Settle Disagreements?
Ephesians 4:26-27

[26]"In your anger do not sin": Do not let the sun go down while you are still angry, [27]and do not give the devil a foothold.

Ephesians 4:26-27

AS WE GROW TOGETHER

Week Nine — Monday
Your Spouse's Love Language
Ephesians 5:22-33

[28]In the same way, husbands ought to love their wives as their own bodies. He who loves his wife loves himself.

Ephesians 5:28

A Prayer Journal for Expectant Couples

Week Nine — Tuesday
Your Family's Mission Statement
Isaiah 32:8

⁸But the noble man makes noble plans, and by noble deeds he stands.
Isaiah 32:8

As We Grow Together

Week Nine — Wednesday
The Plan for the Child's Care
Proverbs 20:18a

[18a] Make plans by seeking advice.

Proverbs 20:18a

A Prayer Journal for Expectant Couples

Week Nine — Thursday
Are We on the Same Page?
2 Corinthians 13:11b, c

[11b, c] Aim for perfection, listen to my appeal, be of one mind, live in peace. And the God of love and peace will be with you.

2 Corinthians 13:11b, c

AS WE GROW TOGETHER

Week Nine — Friday
You and Your Spouse's Communication:
What, When and Where?
Ephesians 4:32; 1 Peter 3:8-9

^{32}Be kind and compassionate to one another, forgiving each other, just as in Christ God forgave you. ^{8}Finally, all of you, live in harmony with one another; be sympathetic, love as brothers, be compassionate and humble. ^{9}Do not repay evil with evil or insult with insult, but with blessings, because to this you were called so that you may inherit a blessing.

Ephesians 4:32; 1 Peter 3:8-9

A Prayer Journal for Expectant Couples

Week Nine — Saturday
You and Your Spouse Communicate: How and Why
Ephesians 4:32; 1 Peter 3:8-9

[32]Be kind and compassionate to one another, forgiving each other, just as in Christ God forgave you. [8]Finally, all of you, live in harmony with one another; be sympathetic, love as brothers, be compassionate and humble. [9]Do not repay evil with evil or insult with insult, but with blessings, because to this you were called so that you may inherit a blessing.

Ephesians 4:32; 1 Peter 3:8-9

_____
_____
_____
_____
_____
_____
_____
_____
_____
_____
_____
_____
_____
_____
_____
_____
_____
_____
_____
_____
_____
_____
_____
_____
_____

As We Grow Together

Week Ten
Your Communication with God
Your individual and collective prayer time with God

I read in a book that if I depended on my husband to be my prayer partner, I would be disappointed. I was disappointed that the book stated that. I realize that the expectation of being my prayer partner is high but I didn't start the expectation. God expected my husband to pray with and for us, first. Then I just used His idea because I liked it. Prayer time with your spouse is truly special and important. I have learned some unique facts that I heard for the first time in front of God. It is awesome to pray with your spouse. It is awesome how close you two can become. It is amazing to watch God in your life and marriage because of your prayers. Prayer with God is essential for the growth between us and Him. Our prayer time should be consistent. Select a specific time of day. Select a place where you and God can commune without interruption.

Prayer is your time to gain complete clarity on your direction. "In all thy ways acknowledge Him and He will direct thy paths." Proverbs 3:6. Seeking God's direction, seeking His face, seeking His voice = humbling ourselves to acknowledge His sovereignty through prayer. Prayer is when you reach solitude, peace, rest and you can leave your burdens with God knowing they will be taken care of.

Finally, prayer is our tool by which we can access His power. His power is very important for us to have. His power is what moves us from our current status of Christianity to new levels where we begin to really experience God and His promises.

Dedicate time to access His power – it's the best investment of your time.

Sunday	Prayer time with God as a Family Isaiah 56:7d
Monday	Reading/Studying God's word as a Family Joshua 1:8, 24:15
Tuesday	Prayer time individually 1 Thessalonians 5:17

A Prayer Journal for Expectant Couples

Wednesday	Study time individually 2 Timothy 2:15
Thursday	How will your child know God – What will you do for your child? Proverbs 22:6
Friday	Prayer Acts: Teaching your child to pray Matthew 6:9-13
Saturday	Prayer Acts: Teaching your child to pray, part 2 Mark 11:24

AS WE GROW TOGETHER

Week Ten — Sunday
Prayer Time with God as Family
Isaiah 56:7d

⁷ᵈFor my house will be called a house of prayer for all nations.
Isaiah 56:7d

A Prayer Journal for Expectant Couples

Week Ten — Monday
Reading/Studying God's Word as a Family
Joshua 1:8; 24:15

⁸Meditate on it day and night, so that you may be careful to do everything written in it. Then you will be prosperous and successful. ¹⁵Then choose for yourselves this day whom you will serve; But as for me and my household we will serve the Lord.

Joshua 1:8; 24:15

_____
_____
_____
_____
_____
_____
_____
_____
_____
_____
_____
_____
_____
_____
_____
_____
_____
_____
_____
_____
_____
_____

AS WE GROW TOGETHER

Week Ten — Tuesday
Prayer Time Individually
1 Thessalonians 5:17

[17]Pray continually.

1 Thessalonians 5:17

A Prayer Journal for Expectant Couples

Week Ten — Wednesday
Study Time Individually
2 Timothy 2:15

[15] Do your best to present yourself to God as an approved, a workman who does not need to be ashamed and who correctly handles the word of truth.

2 Timothy 2:15

As We Grow Together

Week Ten — Thursday
How Will Your Child Know God? – What Will You Do for Your Child?
Proverbs 22:6

⁶Train a child in the way he should go, and when he is old he will not turn from it.

Proverbs 22:6

A Prayer Journal for Expectant Couples

Week Ten — Friday
Prayer: ACTS – Teaching Your Child to Pray, Part 1
Matthew 6:9-13

⁹This, then, is how you should pray: "'Our Father in heaven, hallowed be Your name, ¹⁰Your kingdom come, Your will be done on earth as it is in heaven. ¹¹Give us today our daily bread. ¹²Forgive us our debts, as we also have forgiven our debtors. ¹³And lead us not into temptation, but deliver from the evil one."

Matthew 6:9-13

As We Grow Together

Week Ten — Saturday
Prayer: ACTS – Teaching Your Child to Pray, Part 2
Mark 11:24

[24]Therefore I tell you, whatever you ask for in prayer, believe that you have received it, and it will be yours.

Mark 11:24

A PRAYER JOURNAL FOR EXPECTANT COUPLES

Week Eleven
Pray for Yourself and Your Spouse
The Power of a Praying Wife/Husband
by Stormie Omartian
Col. 4:2-6

Your prayer time is essential for your spiritual growth. There is no time more important than your prayer time. Neglect of your prayer time delays your spiritual growth. In your marriage, prayer is doubly important. Prayer is vital. The success of your marriage hinges on your dedicated, committed and faithful prayer life.

God answers prayers with yes, no, and maybe. Keeping focus on God's wills and desires influences your prayer attitude. Prayer changes your circumstances for the better, also known as God's will. I am committed to my prayer life and sometimes it suffers. Busy schedules. Unrealistic expectations. Children. Work. Church Ministry. All things or events that will interrupt your prayer life if you allow them.

I'm sure that you have developed your prayer requests and thanksgivings, so I will share some suggestions and some of my list: healthy marriage, healthy children, time for myself, quality time with my spouse, Godly instruction for my children, type of wife God called me to be, and Keep Him first. Prayer is your lifeline. Prayer is your source of refuge in your good times and bad.

Sometimes it may be hard for you to remember to pray but it is the best source. Lastly, pray for two additional sources: a prayer partner and a wise married woman of God.

Pray. Pray. Pray.

Sunday	Some Prayer Instructions, Part 1 Colossians 4:2-4
Monday	Some Prayer Instructions, Part 2 Colossians 4:5-6
Tuesday	The Power of a Praying Wife: A Personal Testimony
Wednesday	The Power of a Praying Wife: A Personal Plea Ephesians 3:12

Thursday	The Power of a Praying Husband: A Personal Testimony Ephesians 5:28
Friday	The Power of a Praying Husband: A Personal Plea 1 Peter 3:7
Saturday	The Power of Prayer: 12 Reasons to Pray and Fast

A Prayer Journal for Expectant Couples

Week Eleven — Sunday
Some Prayer Instructions, Part 1
Colossians 4:2-4

²Devote yourselves to prayer, being watchful and thankful. ³And pray for us, too, that God may open a door for our message, so that we may proclaim the mystery of Christ, for which I am in chains. ⁴Pray that I may proclaim it clearly, as I should.

Colossians 4:2-4

As We Grow Together

Week Eleven — Monday
Some Prayer Instructions, Part 2
Colossians 4:5-6

⁵Be wise in the way you act toward outsiders; make the most of every opportunity. ⁶Let your conversation be always full of grace, seasoned with salt, so that you may know how to answer everyone.

Colossians 4:5-6

A Prayer Journal for Expectant Couples

Week Eleven — Tuesday
The Power of a Praying Wife: A Personal Testimony
By Stormie Omartian

The Power of a Praying Wife is indeed powerful. Mrs. Omartian imparts wisdom that is truly marriage-impacting. I read PPW as a single woman because a male friend recommended it. I thought when I started that will be a quick, easy read and all will be well with the world. I began reading and her words changed my entire view on marriage and my role as a spouse. As I read I truly had to consider my position on marriage. I had to decide on how I was going to handle my own issues. Most importantly, how was I going to handle the unknown issues that would arise. The answer is presented clearly: PRAY. Pray often and sacrificially.

As We Grow Together

Week Eleven — Wednesday
The Power of a Praying Wife: A Personal Plea
Ephesians 3:12

[12] In Him and through faith in Him we may approach God with freedom and confidence.

Ephesians 3:12

A Prayer Journal for Expectant Couples

Week Eleven — Thursday
The Power of a Praying Husband: A Personal Testimony
By Stormie Omartian
Ephesians 5:28

[28] In this same way, husbands ought to love their wives as their own bodies. He who loves his wife loves himself.

Ephesians 5:28

As We Grow Together

Week Eleven — Friday
The Power of a Praying Husband: A Personal Testimony
1 Peter 3:7

⁷Husbands, in the same way be considerate as you live with your wives, and treat them with respect as the weaker partner and as heirs with you of the gracious gift of life, so that nothing will hinder your prayers.

1 Peter 3:7

A Prayer Journal for Expectant Couples

Week Eleven — Saturday
The Power of Prayer
12 Reasons to Pray and Fast

12. Prayer is your time to confess with God our sins. He already knows but when we confess, it cleanses and the guilt is eliminated. It is when God forgives us. 2 Ch. 7:14.

11. Prayer is our time to spend time in the awesome presence of God. It is a private, sacred time where God can talk to us and we can tell Him everything, particularly the desires of our hearts. Eph. 6:18.

10. Prayer is a time where we can listen to God. I have decided that while I don't listen in proportion to how much I tell God, eventually He will help me to listen more.

9. Prayer is a time when we intercede for others. God calls us to intercede for others, especially when they ask us. Intercessory prayer is crucial to the needs of others. James 5:16; Job 42:8.

8. Prayer and fasting are companions for spiritual well-being and successful spiritual warfare. Prayer doesn't always accompany fasting, but fasting is always accompanied with prayer. I cannot fast without prayer. Matt. 26:36-46.

7. Fasting eliminates the spiritual space between you and God. We are most at one with Him when fasting. When you eliminate as many objects in your life as possible and focus totally on Him, your relationship increases by leaps and bounds. When I fast, I sacrifice food, television, frivolous conversation and leisure activities in various increments. While you are pregnant, fasting from food is not an option. However, <u>totally</u> eliminating fast food, chips and similarly non-healthy foods from your diet is wise. Matt. 4:1-11.

6. Jesus fasted. As usual, His life as an example overwhelms me, but offers me a clear understanding for what I need to do so that my relationship with God is all that it can be. Matt. 4:5.

5. Prayer provides us the peace we continually search for and request. Phil. 4:7.

As We Grow Together

4. Prayer is where you are freed from your burdens. He said that He would give us rest for those burdened and heavy laden. Matt. 11:28.

3. Prayer is the communication of our faith. We communicate our belief in God and His sovereignty through our prayers.

2. Fasting communicates our seriousness for our relationship with God. He provides us some specific instructions on how to fast, and when it is appropriate. Matt. 6:16-18.

1. Jesus taught us how to pray. God answers us when we pray. Prayer is our lifeline to God. Prayer is crucial to our relationship with God. He calls us to pray. Matt. 6:5-15.

A Prayer Journal for Expectant Couples

Week Twelve
Prayer as a Parent
The Power of a Praying Parent
by Stormie Omartian

As parents, we have been gifted. God doesn't allow everyone to be parents. Not even our friends who we feel deserve to be parents. Why we don't know but it's really not up to us. We are gifted as parents. We are parenting someone who God has also bestowed with gifts. We are parenting the next Christians, the next teachers, attorneys, judges, pastors, the next president, senators, congresspersons, governor. We are trusted with God's messengers. Just imagine what it was like to be Mary, mother of Jesus. Could you have done it? At 12, Jesus was teaching at the synagogue.

Prayer facilitates our conversation with God about what He wants us to do as parents and what He wants us to know about our children. One of my dear friends worked from home when she had her first child. She stopped working after the second child was born. She struggled with the choice but knows it's what God wants her to do. On the other hand, I left my job 3 months before my son was born. I started a home based business after he was born. Then after he turned one, I sought full-time employment while still engaged in my writing, home based business and mothering two and of course, my husband, not to mention my church and my duties there.

Pray over your children. Their well-being is in your hands. We are responsible for them – for the rest of their lives. Prayer is powerful for all that we desire our children to be and to have and to know. Prayer is powerful. I cannot repeat myself enough. Prayer changes attitudes, minds and actions. Keep praying.

Sunday	Praying for Our Children: the Depth of Your Prayer Psalm 6:9
Monday	Praying for Our Children: the Width of Your Prayer Ephesians 6:18
Tuesday	Praying for Our Children: the Territory of Your Prayer Philippians 4:6

Wednesday	Praying for Our Children: the Impact of Your Prayer Matthew 11:25
Thursday	Praying for Our Children: the Best Way to Pray Matthew 26:39
Friday	Praying for Our Children: YOU 2 Thessalonians 1:11-12
Saturday	Praying for Our Children: My Personal Testimony

A Prayer Journal for Expectant Couples

Week Twelve — Sunday
Praying for Our Children
Prayer defined – The Depth of Your Prayer
Psalm 6:9

⁹The Lord has heard my cry for mercy; the Lord accepts my prayer.
Psalm 6:9

What is prayer? Prayer is the discussion with God of our desires, fears, dreams and our children's health, welfare and love. Prayer is our frank conversation with God with the assistance of the Holy Spirit. Prayer is submission to God of all of what burdens us.

_____
_____
_____
_____
_____
_____
_____
_____
_____
_____
_____
_____
_____
_____
_____
_____
_____
_____
_____
_____
_____
_____

AS WE GROW TOGETHER

Week Twelve — Monday
Praying for Our Children
Praying Daily is Required – the Deepness of Your Prayer
Ephesians 6:18

[18] And pray in the Spirit on all occasions with all kinds of prayers and requests. With this in mind, be alert and always keep on praying for all the saints.

Ephesians 6:18

_____
_____
_____
_____
_____
_____
_____
_____
_____
_____
_____
_____
_____
_____
_____
_____
_____
_____
_____
_____
_____
_____
_____
_____

A Prayer Journal for Expectant Couples

Week Twelve — Tuesday
Praying for Our Children
The Territory of Your Prayer
Philippians 4:6

⁶Do not be anxious about anything, but in everything, by prayer and petition, with thanksgiving, present your requests to God.

Philippians 4:6

AS WE GROW TOGETHER

Week Twelve — Wednesday
Praying for Our Children
The Impact of Your Prayers
Matthew 11:25

[25]At that time Jesus said, "I praise You, Father, Lord of heaven and earth, because you have hidden these things from the wise and learned, and revealed them to little children.

Matthew 11:25

A Prayer Journal for Expectant Couples

Week Twelve — Thursday
Praying for Our Children
The Best Way to Pray
Matthew 26:39

[39] Going a little farther, He fell with His face to the ground and prayed, "My Father, if it is possible, may this cup be taken from Me. Yet not as I will, but as You will."

Matthew 26:39

As We Grow Together

Week Twelve — Friday
Praying for Our Children
The Most Important Petitioner for Your Child: YOU
2 Thessalonians 1:11-12

[11] With this in mind, we constantly pray for you, that our God may count you worthy of His calling, and that by His power He may fulfill every good purpose of yours and every act prompted by your faith. [12] We pray this is so that the name of our Lord Jesus may be gloried in you, and you in Him, according to the grace of our God and the Lord Jesus Christ.

2 Thessalonians 1:11-12

_____
_____
_____
_____
_____
_____
_____
_____
_____
_____
_____
_____
_____
_____
_____
_____
_____
_____
_____
_____
_____
_____

A Prayer Journal for Expectant Couples

Week Twelve — Saturday
Praying for Our Children
Power of a Praying Parent – A Personal Testimony
by Stormie Omartian

First, I am a fan of Stormie Omartian and her works. As you remember from earlier weeks, I shared with you the impact of her books. I really hope that you will read her <u>Power of a Praying Parent</u>.

Week Thirteen
Prayers For Your Children

In several weeks, we have alluded to prayer for your children, so we will identify some specific areas of prayer. These areas are a simple sample of the depth and breadth of your prayer life.

Prayer is required for successful parenting as God defines.

Prayer is the most powerful investment in their lives. Prayer also allows you to get what you need to run the parenting marathon. So by all means, pray for yourself, your spouse, your marriage, your life, your family and everything else that concerns you. We live because God supplies life. He provides us a platform for prayer. He expects us to request what we need, and the desires of our heart. This is the definition of comprehensive prayer.

Spend some time examining your current prayer life. Think about ways to extend your prayer life, depth and breadth. Reading about prayer helps develop a passionate prayer life. Joining a prayer ministry fuels your prayer life. These three methods can catapult your prayer life several levels.

My personal method to hold me accountable and to move my prayer life to a higher level is their eyes – her eyes and his eyes. Those two pairs of eyes are all that I need to move the needle in my prayer life. Sometimes when I have fallen from my prayer life, one of them looks at me and causes me to start to pray on the spot, with my eyes open, holding one of them because they need my prayers and my commitment to God. My personal banner for God shows when I least expect it and when I need it most. They cannot read the word for themselves yet so they need me reading, fasting and praying as their intercessor.

I am their prayer warrior. I wrote a poem years ago about a prayer warrior's role. I had no idea then that it would be my role now.

I stand against evil and other forces in their place. My prayers now saves me time for later.

"Mommy?"
"Yes, Hillary?"
Hillary: "Is God talking to me?"
"Yes, Hillary, He is," responds mommy.

A Prayer Journal for Expectant Couples

Sunday	Praying for her spirituality Galatians 5:22-23
Monday	Praying for his actions. Proverbs 20:11
Tuesday	Praying for his obedience Ephesians 6:1; Colossians 3:20
Wednesday	Praying for her knowledge Deuteronomy 4:9
Thursday	Praying for his respect Leviticus 19:3, 32
Friday	Praying for love for and within him 1 Corinthians 13:2a, 13
Saturday	Praying for her future 1 Corinthians 13:11; Jeremiah 29:11; 3 John 2

As We Grow Together

Week Thirteen — Sunday
Praying for Her Spirituality
Galatians 5:22-23, 25

²²But the fruit of the Spirit is love, joy, peace, patience, kindness, goodness, faithfulness, ²³gentleness and self-control. Against such things there is no law. ²⁵Since we live by the Spirit, let us keep in step with the Spirit.

Galatians 5:22-23, 25

A Prayer Journal for Expectant Couples

Week Thirteen — Monday
Praying for His Actions
Proverbs 20:11

[11] Even a child is known by his actions, by whether his conduct is pure and right.

Proverbs 20:11

AS WE GROW TOGETHER

Week Thirteen — Tuesday
Praying for His Obedience
Ephesians 6:1; Colossians 3:20

[1]Children, obey your parents in the Lord, for this is right. [20]Children, obey your parents in everything, for this pleases God.

Ephesians 6:1; Colossians 3:20

A Prayer Journal for Expectant Couples

Week Thirteen — Wednesday
Praying for Her Knowledge
Deuteronomy 4:9

⁹Only be careful, and watch yourselves closely so that you do not forget the things your eyes have seen or let them slip from your heart as long as you live. Teach them to your children and to their children after them.

Deuteronomy 4:9

AS WE GROW TOGETHER

Week Thirteen — Thursday
Praying for His Respect
Leviticus 19:3, 32

³Each of you must respect his mother and father, and you must observe my Sabbaths. I am the Lord your God. ³²Rise in the presence of the aged, show respect for the elderly and revere your God. I am the Lord.
Leviticus 19:3, 32

A Prayer Journal for Expectant Couples

Week Thirteen — Friday
Praying for Love for and Within Him
1 Corinthians 13: 2a, 13

²but have not love, I am nothing. ¹³And now these three remain: faith, hope and love. But the greatest of these is love.

1 Corinthians 13: 2a, 13

AS WE GROW TOGETHER

Week Thirteen — Saturday
Praying for Her Future
1 Corinthians 13:11; Jeremiah 29:11; 3 John 2

[11]When I was a child, I talked like a child, I thought like a child, I reasoned like a child. When I became a man I put away childish ways.
[11]"For I know the plans I have for you," declared the Lord, "plans to prosper you and not to harm you, plans to give you hope and a future.
[2]Dear friend, I pray that you may enjoy good health and that all may go well with you, even as your soul is getting along well.
1 Corinthians 13:11; Jeremiah 29:11; 3 John 2

A Prayer Journal for Expectant Couples

Week Fourteen
Vision
A Game Plan with God's Leadership

Status quo means not exceeding the limits or testing the boundary or going above and beyond to achieve the results. My vision for my family is everything but status quo. Your vision for your family should include strategic plans for fulfilling the purposes God has for us as well as meeting the demands that children bring. This is a great time to investigate your plans for the major benchmarks of her life.

The vision needs to fulfill a purpose. Some events relating to completing the vision will be temporary. A visionary acts without short-sightedness, but rather the long-term effects on some great, yet sacrificial, decisions.

A friend had her son six months after I had Hillary. She took a courageous step in her career and proposed and was approved to work at home. It was important to her that her son be home with her. She made the necessary arrangements for his care when she had away meetings and conferences but most of her work week was with her child at her home. On the other hand I went back to work at my high-profile career, thinking it was important.

Two different decisions. Two families. Two women. I wasn't wrong to return to work but could've made a different decision. Or could I? Different results. What is your vision? What will you do during the different milestones in his life?

Your vision and the related actions starts the legacy you pass on to your children. Because of your choices, you can provide valuable influence to your children while they develop their vision.

The vision you and your spouse share serve critical for the life you now share with a little person. So how will you structure your vision?

What does God have for your vision?

Sunday	Let's Examine the Questions
Monday	Let's Examine the Costs
Tuesday	Personal Testimony – Hillary

As We Grow Together

Wednesday	Personal Testimony – Nehemiah
Thursday	As I Compared Notes
Friday	What is Your Vision Habakkuk 2:2
Saturday	Making It Happen

A PRAYER JOURNAL FOR EXPECTANT COUPLES

Week Fourteen — Sunday
Without Vision the People Will Perish
Let's Examine the Questions

After the bliss and excitement wanes and just before (or during) the morning sickness sets in, there are several questions you need to answer:

(1) What will you name the baby?
(2) Will you find out the gender during the ultrasound?
(3) Who will be the child's guardian parents?
(4) Will you return to work?
(5) If yes, who will care for your child while you are at work?
(6) How long will you stay home with the baby? Do you have enough time at work to take off the time you desire?
(7) Can you work from home? If not full-time, then some days of the week or some half-days?
(8) Can you and your family afford for you to stay home for 6 months? a year? eighteen months?
(9) What happens if you are scheduled off 12 weeks and you don't want to return to work?
(10) How will your life be different with this birth?
(11) When can you employ some help? Parents? Friends? Housekeeper?
(12) How will you raise your child?
(13) Are there any decisions you need to make before the baby arrives?
(14) How will you decorate the nursery? Will it be complete before the baby arrives?
(15) Will you breast feed? If not, which formula? Why?
(16) And other questions which may keep you up at night or wake you very early.

Some of these questions are not critical or life-changing but for those which are, let's examine them. First, pray for wisdom, insight and sound decision-making.

What is your vision?

_____
_____
_____

A Prayer Journal for Expectant Couples

Week Fourteen — Monday
Let's Examine the Costs

There are costs associated with the life changing event. What are these costs? Starting with question four, "Will you return to work?" If you say no, can you adjust to be without that income? Can you replace that income within four to six months? Can you generate that income from home? Can you live without your benefits? Can your husband's benefits cover the family? Can you be completely out of debt before the baby arrives? Your 401k contributions will stop. Can you increase your husband's contributions to not lose the gains for the retirement plan? After the increased deductions, can you live on the one salary? Can you take an extended leave which secures your position for the length of time you want to stay at home in lieu of leaving completely?

_____
_____
_____
_____
_____
_____
_____
_____
_____
_____
_____
_____
_____
_____
_____
_____
_____
_____
_____

AS WE GROW TOGETHER

Week Fourteen — Tuesday
Some Personal Testimony

When we conceived Hillary, I had recently accepted a promotion. I thought it was great. I was wrong. I stayed home for eight weeks. We were on the road as soon as I could drive. I recall her giving back her milk as I was trying to get my eyes examined. During those eight weeks, I was lonely and alone. All the arrangements and help I thought I had failed. I had little sleep. It was a notable disaster.

A Prayer Journal for Expectant Couples

Week Fourteen — Wednesday
Personal Testimony, Part 2

Nehemiah gave me more trouble during the pregnancy than Hillary, but the outcome was different. I stayed home for 3 months with Nehemiah. When I started a new position, he went to a home sitter. Simultaneously, I started a new home-based business, and published two new books. Now the home sitter was okay, not exactly the blessing I counted on. So we changed to a school for three months, in between those arrangements he stayed with me. He could stay with me because my home-based business allows me the flexibility to change at that moment. Besides I had learned from Hillary the importance of choice.

AS WE GROW TOGETHER

Week Fourteen — Thursday
As I Compare Notes

At the top of every mother's list is the best for my kids at whatever cost. Then we stamp "SACRIFICE" on each subsequent item on the list.

I referred earlier to a friend who worked from home when she birthed her son. She already had a daughter who was older. Then on the exact day I had Nehemiah she birthed a daughter. She did the impossible – she QUIT her job. She cited the reason of it was best for my family. It was never her initial vision but it's what is best for her family. Could you quit your job? Leave your career?

_____
_____
_____
_____
_____
_____
_____
_____
_____
_____
_____
_____
_____
_____
_____
_____
_____
_____
_____
_____
_____

A Prayer Journal for Expectant Couples

Week Fourteen — Friday
The Family Vision and the Family Mission Statement
Habakkuk 2:2

²The Lord answered me, "Write the vision."

Habakkuk 2:2

AS WE GROW TOGETHER

Week Fourteen — Saturday
Making It Happen

As I said earlier, these are the hardest working 18 years of your life. This is a short window which seems so long. You decide on the vision, then you have to develop an action plan.

Week Fifteen
Vision
The Financial Strategy

Part of your vision will include a new financial strategy. With the birth of a new baby, there will be budget changes. You need to discuss how to plan for the school, diapers, formula, wipes and all other necessities. Most couples are unaware of the costs associated with a baby. We have to consider the costs (Hillary hadn't arrived yet). All costs are not financial though. On my first Mother's Day, my mother asked me why she had to go to daycare and I commented that we couldn't afford for me to stay at home. I asked her if she could stay at home and keep her and she said no. Sometimes the cost is personal sacrifice and are you willing to sacrifice for the good of the children.

From my personal experiences I have decided that I need to be in a financial situation when I have grandchildren to do what I had wanted to happen for me. I don't always think I can afford the "best" option but I really have decided that I can't afford not to choose the "best" option and readjust the budget.

So what will be affected more than your money? Your time. Your leisure activities. Keep that in mind as you plan. Be prepared for the unexpected. I planned to breast feed. It didn't work as long as I wanted it to work. I introduced formula sooner than I planned to my children and to my budget.

Do your research. Ask God. Ask your friends. Develop the plan. Be ready and willing for any changes that may need to occur.

Don't forget to support each other as these life changes occur. You will need more compassion for one another than you ever have. Ephesians 4:32 is a starting point for developing this needed increase of compassion.

Lastly, the budget is not firm. It is a guide. Write it in pencil.

Sunday   Your Attitude About Money
                    Malachi 3:10

Monday   Your New Financial Plan

Tuesday   New Expenses to Expect

As We Grow Together

Wednesday	Can I Stay at Home
Thursday	The Debt-Free Plan
Friday	Maintain Your Lifestyle Perks
Saturday	Your Insurance Plans

A Prayer Journal for Expectant Couples

Week Fifteen — Sunday
Your Attitude About Money
Malachi 3:10

[10]"Bring the whole tithe into the storehouse, that there may be food in my house. Test me in this," says the Lord Almighty, "and see if I will not throw open the floodgates of heaven and pour out so much blessing that you will not have room enough for it.

Malachi 3:10

AS WE GROW TOGETHER

Week Fifteen — Monday
Your New Financial Plan

The family needs a family plan. This new plan will include additional life insurance, medical coverage and expenses (babies go to the doctor 10 times in the next 2 years) barring any illnesses in between regular checkups and immunizations, child care, medicines, formula, clothes and the list goes on and on.

A Prayer Journal for Expectant Couples

Week Fifteen — Tuesday
New Expenses to Expect

New expenses include diapers, wipes, baby wash, baby lotion, baby shampoo, baby oil, formula, cereal, juice, school tuition, clothes, school uniforms, jar baby food, crib, dresser, photos, photo albums, photo frames, doctor's visits, co-pays, medication, vitamins, bedding, room decorations, music DVD's, educational tools, etc. I could make the list longer.

As We Grow Together

Week Fifteen — Wednesday
Can I Stay at Home?
How Can We Afford for My Wife to Stay Home?

Do you desire to stay with your child(ren)? Do you desire for your wife to be able to stay home? If this is your desire, then you have some preparation to do.

A Prayer Journal for Expectant Couples

Week Fifteen — Thursday
The Debt-Free Plan
Lenders and Not Borrowers

I was not smart enough to complete this process prior to our first child. However, try to get this done as soon as possible.

The debt-free plan frees you up to work on the great aspects of marriage and parenting.

AS WE GROW TOGETHER

Week Fifteen — Friday
Maintain Your Lifestyle Perks

Consider the budget you will now have. Daycare alone will be at least $500 per month. Consider a conservative approach. You still want to be able to have date night. Your quality time with each other is of the utmost importance. Do <u>everything</u> you can to manage your expenses so that you can still afford date night and the "special" gifts.

A Prayer Journal for Expectant Couples
Week Fifteen — Saturday
Your Insurance Plans

I spent several weeks analyzing my insurance plans after I had my son. My auto insurance need to be increased so I increased the coverage, changed companies for a lower rate and found out about all possible discounts. Also at the end of each year between Christmas and the New Year, I will take a defensive driving course for $25 which will save me $200 per year and improve my driving rating for the lowest possible prices.

Week Sixteen
Love
God's Definition

The definition of love is so clear that Paul delivers through God's instruction he left no room for dispute or discussion. The definition is absolute and finite and infinite and fluid all at the same time. God has a way with words, doesn't He? Paul shares so well what God gave him.

Our charge is that we do the same. Life just doesn't happen. Our steps are ordered. God has predetermined plans for us. God has the ultimate love. He loves us in so many ways – always better than we love ourselves.

Our challenge is living as these scriptures say. Go to 1 Corinthians 13 and replace "love" with your name. After you replace your name, read the verses slowly and aloud. Did they make you feel different? Did the sound of your voice convict you in your weak areas? When I did this the first time, I cried after the first few verses. I was so convicted by the Holy Spirit that I cried for ten minutes.

Our next step is to access the power of love. Love is powerful enough to change minds, hearts, souls and actions. How we access that power is also ordered by God. We are not strong enough to love correctly on our own. The Holy Spirit provides us the powerful access that we need for loving others as commanded. What does that power look like and feel like? Well, as a parent, it is important that we are in a comfortable love disposition. Your love tank levels will directly impact how you show and share love with your mate and children.

It is when your love tank is nearly empty, completely empty or past empty that your access to the Holy Spirit and His power to access love at its deepest and most meaningful level.

1 Corinthians 13 fully defines love. If we get 25% of the definition correct, then we have really accomplished something.

Sunday	Excellence Defined 1 Corinthians 12:31
Monday	What is Life Without Love 1 Corinthians 13:1-3

A Prayer Journal for Expectant Couples

Tuesday	Love is a Noun 1 Corinthians 13:4-5
Wednesday	Love is a Verb 1 Corinthians 13:6-7
Thursday	Love Exceeds Our Abilities 1 Corinthians 13:8-10
Friday	Love Exceeds Our Expectations 1 Corinthians 13:11-12
Saturday	The Greatest Characteristic: Love Greater than all Others 1 Corinthians 13:13

<u>Appendix</u>:

When we are love – place your name in the blank.

As We Grow Together

Week Sixteen — Sunday
Excellence Defined
1 Corinthians 12:31

[31]But eagerly desire the greater gifts. And now I will show you the most excellent way.

1 Corinthians 12:31

A Prayer Journal for Expectant Couples
Week Sixteen — Monday
What is Life Without Love
1 Corinthians 13:1-3

¹If I speak in the tongues of men and of angels, but have not love, I am only a resounding gong or a clanging cymbal. ²If I have the gift of prophecy and can fathom all mysteries and all knowledge, and if I have a faith that can move mountains, but have not love, I am nothing. ³If I give all I possess to the poor and surrender my body to the flames, but have not love, I gain nothing.

1 Corinthians 13:1-3

As We Grow Together
Week Sixteen — Tuesday
Love is a Noun
1 Corinthians 13:4-5

⁴Love is patient, love is kind. It does not envy, it does not boast, it is not proud. ⁵It is not rude, it is not self-seeking, it is not easily angered, it keeps no record of wrongs.

1 Corinthians 13:4-5

A Prayer Journal for Expectant Couples

Week Sixteen — Wednesday
Love is a Verb
1 Corinthians 13:6-7

⁶Love does not delight in evil, but rejoices with the truth. ⁷It always protects, always trusts, always hopes, always perseveres.

1 Corinthians 13:6-7

AS WE GROW TOGETHER

Week Sixteen — Thursday
Love Exceeds our Abilities
1 Corinthians 13:8-10

⁸Love never fails. But where there are prophecies, they will cease; where there are tongues, they will be stilled; where there is knowledge, it will pass away. ⁹For we know in part and we prophesy in part, ¹⁰but when perfection comes, the imperfect disappears.

1 Corinthians 13:8-10

A Prayer Journal for Expectant Couples
Week Sixteen — Friday
Love Exceeds Our Expectations
1 Corinthians 13:11-12

[11] When I was a child, I talked like a child, I thought like a child, I reasoned like a child. When I became a man, I put childish ways behind me. [12] Now we see but a poor reflection as in a mirror; then we shall see face to face. Now I know in part; then I shall know fully, even as I am fully known.

1 Corinthians 13:11-12

As We Grow Together

Week Sixteen — Saturday
Greater than All Others
1 Corinthians 13:13

[13] And now these three remain: faith, hope and love. But the greatest of these is love.

1 Corinthians 13:13

Week Seventeen
Love: God Exhibits His Love

God shows repeatedly that He loves us. He created the world. He created us in His image. He saved us. He gives us gifts. He blesses us beyond belief. He plans for our future.

Daily. He loves us daily – all day long.

How do you know God loves you? How do you tell others that God loves you? Does God's love for you elevate your love for yourself?

Based on all that God does, how will you use His exhibition to develop your own love life which you share with your spouse, family, others, and most importantly, your child? How will you show them discipline? How will they know that you love them?

My daughter knows how I love her when I welcome her to sit in my lap, when I read to her, when she climbs in bed next to me and we watch "Blue's Clues," and when we laugh and smile together. She likes to touch my arm and twirl my hair. She likes to put her head on my shoulder just when I'm "busy."

We are God's children and all we want is His time and His attention. Our children want the same time and attention. I received an email once about a little boy who wanted to spend time with his dad but he was always working. One day after asking the same question and getting the same answer, he asked his dad how much he made an hour at work. His dad responded that he made $20 an hour.

The son went to his room and returned with a $20 bill and handed it to his father, saying now can you spend time with me.

Whether this story was true or not I'll never know but the sentiment is happening daily all over the world. How will we allocate time for our gifts – our children – who crave our time and energy? How will they know through the time they spend with you, your views and ideas? How will they know what is right and wrong with your presence? Time with you is valuable and <u>required</u>.

How will you love your child?
How will your child know that you love them?

Sunday   His Love and Our Children

As We Grow Together

John 14:15, 21, 23, 24a

Monday	The Ultimate Gift of Love John 3:16
Tuesday	The Refuge God Provides Psalm 46:1
Wednesday	Our Knowledge of God Psalm 46:10
Thursday	God Forgives Us Psalm 103:3
Friday	Could You Do It? Psalm 103:10-12
Saturday	For Great is His Love Psalm 117:2

A Prayer Journal for Expectant Couples

Week Seventeen — Sunday
His Love and Our Obedience
John 14:15, 21, 23, 24a

[15] If you love me, you will obey what I command. [21] Whoever has my commands and obeys them, he is the one who loves me.
[23] Jesus replied, "If anyone loves me, he will obey my teaching. My father will love him, and we will come to him and make our home with him. [24] He who does not love me will not obey my teaching.

John 14:15, 21, 23, 24a

_____
_____
_____
_____
_____
_____
_____
_____
_____
_____
_____
_____
_____
_____
_____
_____
_____
_____
_____
_____
_____
_____
_____

Week Seventeen — Monday
The Ultimate Gift of Love
John 3:16

[16]For God so loved the world that He gave His one and only Son, that whoever believes in Him shall not perish but have eternal life.

John 3:16

A Prayer Journal for Expectant Couples

Week Seventeen — Tuesday
The Refuge God Provides
Psalm 46:1

[1]God is our refuge and strength, an ever-present help in trouble.

Psalm 46:1

AS WE GROW TOGETHER

Week Seventeen — Wednesday
Our Knowledge of God
Psalm 46:10

[10]Be still and know that I am God.

Psalm 46:10

Week Seventeen — Thursday
God Forgives Us
Psalm 103:3

³who forgives all your sins and heals all your diseases.

Psalm 103:3

As We Grow Together

Week Seventeen — Friday
Could You Do It?
Psalm 103:10-12

[10] He does not treat us as our sins deserve or repay us according to our iniquities. [11] For as high as the heavens are above the earth, so great is His love for those who fear Him; [12] as far as the east is from the west, so far has He removed our transgressions from us.

Psalm 103:10-12

A Prayer Journal for Expectant Couples

Week Seventeen — Saturday
For Great Is His Love
Psalm 117:2

²For great is his love towards us, and the faithfulness of the Lord endures forever.

Psalm 117:2

As We Grow Together

Week Eighteen
Loving Your Spouse

Ephesians is one of the most awesome books of the Bible. Paul outlines life lessons we will need forever. He examines several topics but the one we will focus on is loving your spouse.

Loving your spouse may not be easy. There are many reasons why. On the other hand, your spouse is there for you to love. Paul outlines some critical aspects of that love. He clearly explains God's expectations of that relationship and your love. Loving your spouse makes it easier to love your child. God designed your spouse for you to love. Your spouse should know you love him or her. Your spouse should feel and see your love. Mostly, your spouse will experience your love. Loving your spouse is a full-time, vacation-free, selfless, timeless and eternal commitment.

Further, marriage is a no-assumption zone. Neither of you can afford to make any assumptions. In relation to your marriage, assumptions create havoc. In your relation to your children and your marriage, making assumptions create triple the havoc.

Your child will challenge you and press you at difficult moments but do not neglect the house rules. If we haven't covered house rules, there are some.

We moved off the subject somewhat but it is critical that we understand how to love our spouse.

The enemy attempts attacks on us through those we love the most. It is wise to understand that and prepare for that. Now the start of that love is described as openly, honestly, fully, completely, sacrificially and eternally.

Does your spouse _experience_ your love? If you are not sure, then we need to make some adjustments. Don't worry, pilots make in-flight adjustments all the time and they arrive at their destination and most often on time.

Sunday	Who loves like that? Ephesians 5:25-26
Monday	How does this work exactly? Ephesians 5:27-28

A Prayer Journal for Expectant Couples

Tuesday	Where are the scissors? Ephesians 5:31
Wednesday	The Misconception of the Dirty Word Ephesians 5:22
Thursday	God holds him responsible Ephesians 5:23
Friday	"In Everything" Ephesians 5:24b
Saturday	Till Death Do Us Part – Love

As We Grow Together

Week Eighteen — Sunday
Who Loves Like That?
Ephesians 5:25-26

^{25}Husbands, love your wives, just as Christ loved the Church and gave himself up for her ^{26}to make her holy, cleansing her by the washing with water through the word.

Ephesians 5:25-26

A Prayer Journal for Expectant Couples

Week Eighteen — Monday
How Does This Work Exactly?
Ephesians 6:27-28

^{27}and to present her to himself as a radiant church, without stain or wrinkle or any other blemish, but holy and blameless. ^{28}In this same way, husbands ought to love their wives as their own bodies. He who loves his wife loves himself.

Ephesians 6:27-28

Week Eighteen — Tuesday
Where Are the Scissors?
Ephesians 5:31

³¹"For this reason a man will leave his father and mother and be united to his wife, and the two will become one flesh."

Ephesians 5:31

A Prayer Journal for Expectant Couples

Week Eighteen — Wednesday
The Misconception of the Dirty Word
Ephesians 5:22

[22] Wives, submit to your husbands as to the Lord.

Ephesians 5:22

As We Grow Together

Week Eighteen — Thursday
God Holds Him Responsible
Ephesians 5:23

²³For the husband is the head of the wife as Christ is the head of the church, his body, of which he is the Savior.

Ephesians 5:23

A Prayer Journal for Expectant Couples

Week Eighteen — Friday
"In Everything"
Ephesians 5:24b

[24b]Now as the church submits to Christ, so also wives should submit to their husbands <u>in everything</u>.

Ephesians 5:24b

As We Grow Together

Week Eighteen — Saturday
Till Death Do Us Part – Love

Your spouse needs to experience your love. She needs to experience your love in her love language. He needs to feel your love.

Week Nineteen
Loving Your Spouse

Experience requires time. Nothing is perfected overnight but over time. Set aside or schedule quality time with your spouse. You are not courting anymore so you no longer drop everything because she wants ice cream from the parlor across town. Or miss your favorite show because she wants to talk.

So how do you love your spouse with child(ren), or one(s) on the way, financial boundaries, family obligations, church, work, and on the list goes?

In the next several pages, we will address how to love your spouse, how to ask the tough questions, how to move from behind your pride to forgive so that you are equipped to love. We will give specifics along with an appendix of resources for more suggestions.

Keeping up with this fast, microwave lifestyle can be challenging. You need to remember we are here to please and glorify God. Everything we do should align itself with the word of God. Some of those "things" that stop us from spending time with our spouses should be completely eliminated from our lifestyles.

After you ask your mate, then ask yourself what is distracting you from loving your spouse. Secondly, ask yourself what 'can you do to love your spouse more actively and effectively.'

I mentioned overtime earlier in reference to a length of time but also overtime referencing more time than you may consider as enough to continue your relationship. Sometimes overtime is required.

I will advise you to do all the things that you did to attract your mate in order to keep your mate. That advice would serve well to both spouses. Be honest and be prepared to make some changes. Wisdom dictates that you and your spouse reserve some renewal time for your relationship. Date nights need to be weekly, not longer than bi-weekly. Weekend travel needs to happen quarterly. Marriage retreats need to occur when they are offered, no fewer than semi-annually. These times will require your creativity. You will have children to find care for and you will need 3 plans for each occasion.

Make time to love your spouse.

AS WE GROW TOGETHER

Sunday	How to Love Your Spouse
Monday	How to Be Lovable for Your Spouse
Tuesday	Asking the Tough Questions Matthew 18:15-17; Luke 17:3-4
Wednesday	Forgiveness Equips Us to Love Ephesians 4:32; Matthew 6:14-15; 1 Corinthians 13:5
Thursday	Define Your Love
Friday	Define the Capacities You will Serve God
Saturday	Define Your Roles . . . Again

A Prayer Journal for Expectant Couples

Week Nineteen — Sunday
How to Love Your Spouse

Loving your spouse can be difficult but doesn't have to be. I will make several points that may need to be tailored specifically to your spouse, but the main point is taking the time to do something positive to make positive results in your marriage.

As We Grow Together

Week Nineteen — Monday
How to Be Lovable to Your Spouse

We discussed how to love your spouse. Now how do you receive that love? How do you entice those actions? How do you welcome those actions? The following list will, in many ways, complement the previous one.

A Prayer Journal for Expectant Couples

Week Nineteen — Tuesday
Asking the Tough Questions

Nothing feeds tension between a couple like not being able to ask a tough question. Tough questions need to be answered . . . immediately. Resolving these issues insures that you keep your communication lines open.

As We Grow Together

Week Nineteen — Wednesday
Forgiveness Equips us to Love
Ephesians 4:32; Matthew 6:14-15

³²Be kind and compassionate to one another, forgiving each other, just as Christ Gad forgave you.
¹⁴For if you forgive men when they sin against you, your heavenly Father will also forgive you. ¹⁵But if you do not forgive men their sins, your Father will not forgive your sins.

Ephesians 4:32; Matthew 6:14-15

Week Nineteen — Thursday
Define Your Love

How long will your love last? How will you express love? How will you resolve conflict? What is your love based on? How do you define your love?

Do you have any house rules? For example, do you go to bed angry or not?

AS WE GROW TOGETHER
Week Nineteen — Friday
Define the Capacities In Which You will Serve God

We discussed a family and couple's mission statement. If you still haven't done it, it's time.

_____
_____
_____
_____
_____
_____
_____
_____
_____
_____
_____
_____
_____
_____
_____
_____
_____
_____
_____
_____
_____
_____
_____
_____
_____

A Prayer Journal for Expectant Couples

Week Nineteen — Saturday
Define Your Roles . . . Again

What do you want your marriage to look like?

What does it take to make that work?

Your ideal marriage and the reality will be different but by how much is the difference. The measure of this difference will be the measure of your success.

Week Twenty
Love Yourself

Congratulations! You are about to be the proud parents of a wonderful baby. Hats off to you for accepting God's gift of parenting! He doesn't choose everyone to parent.

By the way, your job description just changed . . . dramatically, to say the least.

First things first: take care of yourself. Renew, revive, and rejuvenate yourself as often as possible. Babies change your ability to care for yourself.

On the other side of that, babies require love! No, you won't run out but do you love yourself enough to unselfishly love this baby whose very existence depends on your love-ability.

FACT: babies grow faster and healthier when they are held. They thrive when they are hugged and held. Premature babies when held early and often gain their body weight, strength and health.

Further, when twins are both struggling to hold on to life, in order to help their survival chances they put them in the incubator together.

LOVE is <u>required</u>! We are in week 20. You have 18 weeks to build your love tank, self-esteem and love-ability. Find out what makes your love ability grow. Find out what makes you thrive. Invest in yourself. Believe in yourself! Love yourself! You are designed to love! Your love list: God, your spouse, your children, your family, other Christians, other people who need Jesus and YOURSELF!!!

Start working on loving yourself more. Read, go to workshops, counseling and any other mechanisms. ASK God and read His word.

Similar to sharing your body with your child, you will need to share how to love with your child. I am not leaving love lessons for my child in the hands of the world.

Loving yourself is not easy but can be attained and maintained with God's help. Loving yourself is quite rewarding beyond measure.

A PRAYER JOURNAL FOR EXPECTANT COUPLES

Sunday	Love Yourself Defined: What loving yourself means; What God says. Psalm 139:14; Genesis 1:27; Deuteronomy 6:5
Monday	Love Yourself Defined: What it does not mean 1 Corinthians 13:4-7
Tuesday	Why Loving Yourself is so important Ephesians 5:29
Wednesday	What Steps Can I take to Love Myself Galatians 5:22-23
Thursday	Love Yourself Unconditionally: Forgiveness Matthew 18:21-22; 6:12
Friday	Love Yourself Purposely: Mission/Vision Jeremiah 29:11
Saturday	Love Yourself Properly: Your Health at its Best 3 John 2

As We Grow Together

Week Twenty — Sunday
Love Yourself Defined: What God says about Loving Yourself
Psalm 139:14; Genesis 1:27; Deuteronomy 6:5

[14]"You are fearfully and wonderfully made."
[27]"So God created human beings in His own image. In the image of God He created them; male and female He created them."
[5]"And you must love the Lord your God with all your heart, all your soul and all your strength."

Psalm 139:14; Genesis 1:27; Deuteronomy 6:5

A Prayer Journal for Expectant Couples

Week Twenty — Monday
Love Yourself Defined: What It Does Not Mean
1 Corinthians 13:4-7

⁴Love is patient, love is kind, and is not jealous; love does not brag and is not arrogant, ⁵does not act unbecomingly; it does not seek its own, is not provoked, does not take into account a wrong suffered, ⁶does not rejoice in unrighteousness, but rejoices with the truth; ⁷bears all things, believes all things, hopes all things, endures all things.

1 Corinthians 13:4-7

AS WE GROW TOGETHER

Week Twenty — Tuesday
Why Loving Yourself is so Important
Ephesians 5:29

[29]For no one ever hated his own flesh, but nourishes and cherishes it, just as Christ also does the church.

Ephesians 5:29

A Prayer Journal for Expectant Couples

Week Twenty — Wednesday
Love Yourself: The Essential Steps
Galatians 5:22-23

[22]But the fruit of the Spirit is love, joy, peace, patience, kindness, goodness, faithfulness, [23]gentleness, self-control; against such things there is no law.

Galatians 5:22-23

AS WE GROW TOGETHER

Week Twenty — Thursday
Love Yourself Unconditionally: Forgiveness
Matthew 6:12; 18:21-22

¹²And forgive us our debts, as we also have forgiven our debtors. ²¹Then Peter came and said to Him, "Lord, how often shall my brother sin against me and I forgive him? Up to seven times?" ²²Jesus said to him, "I do not say to you, up to seven times, but up to seventy times seven."

Matthew 6:12; 18:21-22

_____
_____
_____
_____
_____
_____
_____
_____
_____
_____
_____
_____
_____
_____
_____
_____
_____
_____
_____
_____
_____
_____
_____
_____
_____

A Prayer Journal for Expectant Couples

Week Twenty — Friday
Love Yourself Purposely: Mission and Vision
Jeremiah 29:11

[11]"For I know the plans that I have for you," declares the Lord, plans for welfare and not for calamity to give you a future and a hope.

Jeremiah 29:11

_____
_____
_____
_____
_____
_____
_____
_____
_____
_____
_____
_____
_____
_____
_____
_____
_____
_____
_____
_____
_____
_____
_____
_____
_____

As We Grow Together

Week Twenty — Saturday
Love Yourself Properly: Your Health at its Best
3 John 2

²Beloved, I pray that in all respects you may prosper and be in good health, just as your soul prospers.

3 John 2

Week Twenty-One
Love Yourself

Love yourself with the fruit of the Spirit. If we haven't said so already, loving yourself is crucial to loving your child.

The fruit allows you to do the unimaginable, like love others, walk away from temptation and exercise good will with yourself and others. The nine characteristics of the fruit are treated separately but operate as a unit. They all need to work together within us to be the product of the Spirit. As we walk through each element of the fruit, we will examine life instances where this characteristic comes into practice.

Having spiritual fruit grants us access to the Father, Jesus and the Holy Spirit. With this access, we gain power of influence in our interactions and relationships. We are only granted this power because we will not misuse its value. As with any power, there is also accountability. We are now completely knowledgeable about our accountability to the Holy Spirit because we are equipped to handle the situations with which we are presented.

Now, the fruit is love, joy, peace, patience, kindness, goodness, faithfulness, gentleness and self-control. The elements are co-dependent and co-existent. We may not have them to the same degree but they are proportional. For example if we measured the amount with 10 being the max, I would not be a 10 in love and a 1 in gentleness. How will people view you as love or loving if you are harsh or rude? You will have them in proportion and in order. As one or several strengthen, they will all strengthen. If one area is weak, they are all considered weak.

Pick a starting point for your fruit work and move the fruit toward the spirit.

Now, each element of the fruit needs attention so we will discuss them individually. The fruit which you bear announces itself as it grows. Fruit also has a self-replenishment factor so that you will not run out. As a matter of fact, the more of the fruit you share, the more fruit you will be able to share.

Sunday   Love: Membership Leadership Has its Privileges
             Galatians 5:22; John 3:16

As We Grow Together

Monday	Joy: A Measure of Wealth Galatians 5:22; James 1:2
Tuesday	Peace: Not a Choice, a Provision Galatians 5:22; Philippines 4:7; 1 Corinthians 7:15; Colossians 3:15
Wednesday	Patience: Can you do the same Galatians 5:22; 1 Thessalonians 5:14
Thursday	Kindness Galatians 5:22; Ephesians 4:32
Friday	Goodness Galatians 5:22; Matthew 12:35
Saturday	Faithfulness Galatians 5:22; Hebrews 11:6

A Prayer Journal for Expectant Couples

Week Twenty-One — Sunday
Love: From Privileged Beginnings
Galatians 5:22-23; John 3:16

²²But the fruit of the Spirit is love. ¹⁶For God so loved the world that He gave His one and only Son, that whoever believes in Him shall not perish but have eternal life.

Galatians 5:22; John 3:16

As We Grow Together

Week Twenty-One — Monday
Joy: A Measure of Wealth
Galatians 5:22; James 1:2

²²But the fruit of the Spirit is love, joy, ²Consider it pure joy, my brothers, whenever you face trials of many kinds.

Galatians 5:22; James 1:2

_____
_____
_____
_____
_____
_____
_____
_____
_____
_____
_____
_____
_____
_____
_____
_____
_____
_____
_____
_____
_____
_____
_____
_____
_____

A Prayer Journal for Expectant Couples

Week Twenty-One — Tuesday
Peace: A Provision, Not a Choice
Galatians 5:22; Philippians 4:7; 1 Corinthians 7:15b; Colossians 3:15

[22] But the fruit of the Spirit is love, joy, peace.
[15b] God has called us to live in peace.
[7] And the peace of God, which transcends all understanding, will guard your hearts and your minds in Christ Jesus.
[15] Let the peace of Christ rule in your hearts, since as members of one body you were called to peace. And be thankful.

Galatians 5:22; Philippians 4:7; 1 Corinthians 7:15b; Colossians 3:15

Week Twenty-One — Wednesday
Patience: Can I expect the same from you?
Galatians 5:22-23; 1 Thessalonians 5:14

[22]But the fruit of the Spirit is love, joy, peace, patience
[14]And we urge you, brothers, warn those who are idle, encourage the timid, help the weak, be patient with everyone.

Galatians 5:22; 1 Thessalonians 5:14

A PRAYER JOURNAL FOR EXPECTANT COUPLES

Week Twenty-One — Thursday
Kindness: The Golden Rule Updated
Galatians 5:22-23; Ephesians 4:32

[22]But the fruit of the Spirit is love, joy, peace, patience, kindness
[32]Be kind and compassionate to one another, forgiving each other, just as in Christ God forgave you.

Galatians 5:22; Ephesians 4:32

As We Grow Together
Week Twenty-One — Friday
Goodness
Galatians 5:22-23; Timothy 6:18

²²But the fruit of the Spirit is love, joy, peace, patience, kindness, goodness
¹⁸Command them to do good, to be rich in good deeds, and to be generous and willing to share.

Galatians 5:22; Timothy 6:18

A Prayer Journal for Expectant Couples

Week Twenty-One — Saturday
Faithfulness
Galatians 5:22-23; Hebrews 11:6

^{22}But the fruit of the Spirit is love, joy, peace, patience, kindness, goodness, faithfulness
And ^{6}Without faith it is impossible to please God because anyone who comes to him must believe that he exists and that rewards those who earnestly seek him.

Galatians 5:22; Hebrews 11:6

Week Twenty-Two
Love Yourself: The Fruit Continued

We spent last week on the fruit of the Spirit and how they relate. We will continue our study on the last two elements, then we will move on to the Fruit Lifestyle.

These last two elements are by far a challenge for me. They call me to a life of excellence. I have to master them so that I can be an example for my children and their children. Also as I grow closer to Christ, He helps the fruits better active in me. The Spirit desires for the fruits to be active in each of us. In order for that to happen we are required to focus on the Lord daily. Luke 9:23 says that "If any man would come after me, he must take up his cross daily and follow me."

Daily time with God is required. Growing closer to God assures that you grow closer to your loved ones. Daily time is hard to come by sometimes but prioritize His time. His time develops the fruit.

Keep a growth journal for notes on how you've grown as you study.

These last two fruit elements are gentleness and self-control. Certainly, they are not the most difficult yet they are critical to our whole package.

As a leader of my child and as an example for other children, gentleness extends to each life and strengthens relationships. Gentleness builds the self-esteem of others and any exhibit of gentleness is the epitome of what Jesus would do. Also your gentleness encourages others' gentleness. Gentleness is necessary for the growth of the Christian world. Self-control cannot be more important now than ever before. With road rage, crime, and threats of national security, self-control is a commodity and crucial to raising responsible children as citizens. Self-control includes language, overall behavior, how you handle the sales associates to how to handle disagreements with your spouse.

Self-control and discipline are synonymous. Self-control includes eating, driving, education and maintenance and spending.

The fruit of gentleness and self-control truly minister through the whole person to the whole community, which starts at your address.

Sunday   Gentleness Evidence
               Galatians 5:22-23; Philippians 4:5

A Prayer Journal for Expectant Couples

Monday	Self-Control Galatians 5:22-23; Titus 1:8
Tuesday	His Provision and Power/The Power of His Provision 2 Peter 1:3-4
Wednesday	My Homework, Part 1 2 Peter 1:5-6
Thursday	My Homework, Part 2 2 Peter 1:7
Friday	Promises Fulfilled 2 Peter 1:8-9
Saturday	Promises Fulfilled and Complete 2 Peter 1:10-11

As We Grow Together

Week Twenty-Two — Sunday
Gentleness
Galatians 5:22-23; Philippians 4:5

²²But the fruit of the Spirit is love, you, peace, patience, kindness, goodness, faithfulness, ²³gentleness
⁵Let your gentleness be evident to all. The Lord is near.

Galatians 5:22-23; Philippians 4:5

A Prayer Journal for Expectant Couples

Week Twenty-Two — Monday
Self-Control
Galatians 5:22-23; Titus 1:8

[22] But the fruit of the Spirit is love, joy, peace, patience, kindness, goodness, faithfulness, [23] gentleness, and self-control. Against such things there is no law.

[8] Rather he must be hospitable, one who loves what is good, who is self-controlled, upright, holy and disciplined.

Galatians 5:22-23; Titus 1:8

AS WE GROW TOGETHER

Week Twenty-Two — Tuesday
The Power of His Provision
2 Peter 1:3-4

³His divine power has given us everything we need for life and godliness through our knowledge of Him who called us by His own glory and goodness. ⁴Through these He has given us His very great and precious promises, so that through them you may participate in the divine nature and escape the corruption in the world caused by evil desires.

2 Peter 1:3-4

A PRAYER JOURNAL FOR EXPECTANT COUPLES

Week Twenty-Two — Wednesday
My Homework, Part 1
The Prescription for Righteousness Living
2 Peter 1:5-6

⁵For this very reason, make every effort to add to your faith goodness; and to goodness, knowledge; ⁶and to knowledge, self-control; and to self-control, perseverance; and to perseverance, godliness;

2 Peter 1:5-6

As We Grow Together

Week Twenty-Two — Thursday
My Homework, Part 2
2 Peter 1:7

⁷and to godliness, brotherly kindness; and to brotherly kindness, love.

2 Peter 1:7

A Prayer Journal for Expectant Couples
Week Twenty-Two — Friday
Promises Fulfilled
2 Peter 1:8-9

⁸For if you possess these qualities in increasing measure, they will keep you from being ineffective and unproductive in your knowledge of our Lord Jesus Christ. ⁹But if anyone does not have them, he is nearsighted and blind, and has forgotten that he has been cleansed from his past sins.

2 Peter 1:8-9

As We Grow Together

Week Twenty-Two — Saturday
Promises Fulfilled and Complete
2 Peter 1:10-11

¹⁰therefore, my brothers, be all the more eager to make your calling and election sure. For if you do these things, you will never fall, ¹¹and you will receive a rich welcome into the eternal kingdom of our Lord and Savior Jesus Christ.

2 Peter 1:10-11

A Prayer Journal for Expectant Couples

Week Twenty-Three
Taking Care of Yourself: An Act of Love

When I was pregnant with Hillary, our first child, I learned the hard way that taking care of myself is my top and only priority. I know that by now you have realized that you have to eat properly, drink lots of water and take your vitamins. This week we will go further. What are you doing for your emotional and spiritual health and well-being? Are you able to relax and stress free? This should be a pleasant time with some work but not the work which is stressful and not liked.

What do you do to relax? Do you read? Write? Walk? Shop? Spa visits? What do you do that allows you to regroup from your workday?

The ideal show of love is taking care of yourself. Resting, drinking plenty of water, relaxing, monitoring your weight, vitamins, regular exercise, and the spa are all key to your health.

Taking care of yourself is not optional – it is required. Your total person affects the growth and well-being of the baby, and ultimately, your entire family.

I remember several nights when I arrived home, ate dinner and laid down for some rest at seven in the evening and slept until seven the next morning. These twelve hours indicated that I need more rest.

Pay attention to your body. Don't ignore any signs or pains or discomfort or twinges. Your baby and body will help you understand what you need.

I remember my first pregnancy so well that with my second pregnancy, I did a better job taking care of myself. I owed my care to my baby and to my family and to myself. Your body is a temple for Christ to dwell. It is my job to care for myself.

Your health and the health of the baby are not replaceable. Your health is a precious gift you should cherish. Taking care of yourself is the best thank you note you can write to God.

Sunday	Sleep? Who needs it anyway?
Monday	Water – THE necessity
Tuesday	Relaxation. Stop cleaning and sit.

Wednesday	Weight management
Thursday	Vitamins and the Health Diet
Friday	Exercise for the Expectant Couple
Saturday	The Spa: Our Destination

A Prayer Journal for Expectant Couples

Week Twenty-Three — Sunday
Sleep? Who needs it anyway?

You need 9-12 hours of rest each day. Your body replenishes itself during rest and you have more to replenish. You need to sleep now because remember when your bundle of joy arrives you are then on her schedule – not your own.

AS WE GROW TOGETHER

Week Twenty-Three — Monday
Water – THE NECESSITY

64 ounces per day is the minimum. Your body needs hydration. Water is the best form. WATER. Not juice, milk, punch, sports drinks or electrolyte drinks or diet supplements.

A Prayer Journal for Expectant Couples
Week Twenty-Three — Tuesday
Relaxation – Stop cleaning and sit

So relax. Just sit down. Put your feet up for twenty minutes each day. This increases your circulation which prevents future issues.

As We Grow Together

Week Twenty-Three — Wednesday
Weight Management

Begin with the end in mind. Most of us have heard that statement before now, so we will use that to direct us in our weight management.

A Prayer Journal for Expectant Couples

Week Twenty-Three — Thursday
Vitamins and the Healthy Diet

If you recall your first pre-natal visit, you were prescribed vitamins immediately. Vitamins are an important part of your baby's health and your health. I didn't use vitamins prior to my pregnancies, so taking daily medication was somewhat challenging. Chewable vitamins made life easier. I highly recommend them.

As We Grow Together

Week Twenty-Three — Friday
Exercise for the Expectant Couple

Exercise with your spouse is a rewarding time spent together. Walking, yoga and bicycling (not while pregnant – check with your doctor) offer the perfect exercises for bringing you and your spouse together, closer at heart. Make it a fun and romantic time. Most couples won't admit that many obstacles come into their lives which discourage closeness. I want you to know that you need to have many "touch-points" in your marriage. Gage's definition of "touch-points" is points in your marriage where your hearts and bodies touch, physically, emotionally and spiritually.

A Prayer Journal for Expectant Couples
Week Twenty-Three — Saturday
The Spa: Our Destination

Gentlemen, this will be a definite treat. Earlier, I mentioned the prenatal massage. In addition, regular massages are great therapy for you. Massages keep stress low and lower the opportunity for other health issues stress induces. Consider having massages while in the same room. It is a wonderful experience.

Week Twenty-Four
Parent As Teacher

"More is caught than taught" is a phrase that I have heard more lately as a new parent than ever. Being in the new parent club introduces you to personal growth through reflection. You are your child's first teacher and you will be her teacher all of your life. She does what she sees you do and repeats that action or words. He is a reflection of you.

Your child learns everything from you until she starts school and visits others. Be careful, this could be a compliment or a complaint.

Construct your lesson plans carefully. Decide on your parenting rules carefully. Remember once you establish your standards, take a stand for your rules and beliefs. Someone will challenge your rules.

Our rules:

(1) No secular music in front of the children.
(2) Certain words/phrases are not permitted (shut up).
(3) Can chew sugar-free gum.
(4) Proper grammar.
(5) No violent television/movies in front of children.

Remember that we live by these rules before them so we don't create a double standard. Otherwise when you tell your child to do or not to do something, you may hear the words, "But you do it." You won't be able to prevent all instances but those things you feel strong about, you discipline yourself accordingly. My daughter watches us so closely that I am so conscious of my behavior, the good and the not so good. They do what you do. They say what you say. Would you like to see your reflection when it is less than positive?

You are the teacher. You are the model. You are the example. You are the standard. Prepare for the best. Prepare to be outstanding. What is your lesson plan? What is your strategy? Who will assist you? When my children do something that I don't necessarily care for, I call my mother and apologize for doing that to her.

As a parent, I study and pray a lot. Also, I have personally taken some of the limits off of my life. I have enrolled in a master's program for business and will earn two other degrees, one of which is a doctorate. I will do it and expect my children to do the same.

A Prayer Journal for Expectant Couples

Sunday	Salvation
	Romans 10:9-10; Ephesians 2:8-9
Monday	Spiritual Gifts
	Matthew 25:14-30
Tuesday	Love
	John 14:15
Wednesday	Faith
	Hebrews 11:6
Thursday	Tithing and Money
	Malachi 3:10 (8-9)
Friday	Worship and Praise
	John 4:24; Psalm 139:14
Saturday	Peace
	Philippians 4:7

Week Twenty-Four — Sunday
Salvation
Romans 1:9-10; Ephesians 2:8-9

⁹That if you confess with your mouth, "Jesus is Lord," and believe in your heart that God raised him from the dead, you will be saved. ¹⁰For it is with your heart that you believe and are justified, and it is with your mouth that you confess and are saved.
⁸For it is by grace you have been saved, through faith – and this not from yourselves, it is the gift of God – ⁹not by works, so that no one can boast.

Romans 1:9-10; Ephesians 2:8-9

A Prayer Journal for Expectant Couples

Week Twenty- Four — Monday
Spiritual Gifts
Matthew 25:14-30

[18]But the man who had received the one talent went off, dug a hole in the ground and hid his master's money.

Matthew 25:18

As We Grow Together

Week Twenty-Four — Tuesday
Love
John 14:15

[15]If you love me, you will obey what I command.

John 14:15

A Prayer Journal for Expectant Couples

Week Twenty- Four — Wednesday
Faith
Hebrews 11:6

⁶And without faith it is impossible to please God, because anyone who comes to Him must believe that He exists and that He rewards those who earnestly seek Him.

Hebrews 11:6

As We Grow Together

Week Twenty- Four — Thursday
Tithing and Money
Malachi 3:8-10

⁸"Will a man rob God? Yet you rob me." "But you ask, 'How do we rob you?'" "In tithes and offerings. ⁹You are under a curse – the whole nation of you – because you are robbing me. ¹⁰Bring the whole tithe into the storehouse, that there may be food in my house. Test me in this," says the Lord Almighty, "and see if I will not throw open the floodgates of heaven and pour out so much blessing that you will not have room enough for it.

Malachi 3:8-10

A Prayer Journal for Expectant Couples

Week Twenty-Four — Friday
Worship and Praise
John 4:24; Psalm 139:14

[24]"God is spirit, and his worshippers must worship in spirit and in truth."

[14]I praise you because I am fearfully and wonderfully made, your works are wonderful, I know that full well.

John 4:24; Psalm 139:14

As We Grow Together

Week Twenty- Four — Saturday
Peace
Philippians 4:7

[7]And the peace of God, which transcends all understanding, will guard your hearts and minds in Chris Jesus.

Philippians 4:7

A Prayer Journal for Expectant Couples

Week Twenty-Five
Lifestyle Changes

A baby changes your routine. A baby changes everything about your life. Forever. Once that baby arrives, your life will never be the same.

Most men think that it is impossible for that to happen but it is true. Anticipate, expect, and plan for change.

In the areas of home dynamics, career, priorities, goals, money, house rules and decisions and answers, you can expect change. Immediate and definitive.

My priorities definitely changed. My goals changed. When I consider what I wanted out of life for myself, once I had children, now I want more because I want my life to positively influence them. I went back to earn my master's degree. These are all concepts to consider when you consider your life and the life you create for your children and yourself.

Dust off that dream and goal sheet. Chart your progress. Re-ignite that spirit. Remember that your life is defined by more now. A little person with her own personality changes your perspective. He moves your boundaries. He causes you to step up to the plate and do your best in all areas of your life.

During my first pregnancy, the parents of five children approached my table, congratulated me and suggested that I enjoy all of the hot meals, naps and quiet time that I could. He continued by saying that when the baby arrived, most of that would cease. I said thank you graciously and had to carefully consider the timing and delivery of that information. I was initially in doubt or denial about the validity of their information but I consider the source – they had five children. As the parent of five children, I had to admit that they were a credible enough source to share and not be challenged.

There is wisdom in that information and regardless of whether they earned that knowledge or someone else shared it with them, I am passing it on to you with the same intentions they had when they shared.

Sunday   The Family Goals
                  Jeremiah 29:11

Monday   The Home Dynamics

AS WE GROW TOGETHER

Proverbs 31:11, 15, 26, 28; 1 Timothy 3:12

Tuesday	The Family Priorities Joshua 24:15; Matthew 21:13
Wednesday	Your Careers Proverbs 31:16-17, 22a, 24, 27; Ecclesiastes 5:8
Thursday	Money & Its Differences 1 Peter 5:2
Friday	House Rules: Decisions: How are they made? Ephesians 5:17, 23
Saturday	House Rules: Answers: Who has them? Ephesians 4:26-27; 5:21

A Prayer Journal for Expectant Couples

Week Twenty-Five — Sunday
The Family Goals
Jeremiah 29:11

[11]"For I know the plans I have for you," declares the Lord, "plans to prosper you and not to harm you, plans to give you hope and a future."

Jeremiah 29:11

As We Grow Together

Week Twenty-Five — Monday
The Home Dynamics
Proverbs 31:11, 15, 26 & 28; 1 Timothy 3:12

¹¹Her husband has full confidence in her and lacks nothing of value.
²⁸Her children arise and called her blessed; her husband also, and he praises her.
¹²A deacon must be the husband of but one wife and must manage his children and his household well.

Proverbs 31:11 & 28; 1 Timothy 3:12

A Prayer Journal for Expectant Couples
Week Twenty-Five — Tuesday
The Family Priorities
Joshua 24:15b; Matthew 21:13a

[15b]But as for me and my household, we will serve the Lord.
[13a]"It is written," he said to them, "My house will be called a house of prayer."

Joshua 24:15b; Matthew 21:13a

AS WE GROW TOGETHER

Week Twenty-Five — Wednesday
Your Careers
Proverbs 31:16-17, 22a, 24, 27; Ecclesiastes 5:10

¹⁶She considers a field and buys it; out of her earnings she plants a vineyard. ¹⁷She sets about her work vigorously; her arms are strong for her tasks. ²²ᵃShe makes coverings for her bed; ²⁴she makes linen garments and sells them, and supplies the merchant with sashes. ²⁷She watches over the affairs of her household and does not eat the bread of idleness.

¹⁰Whoever loves money never had money enough; whoever loves wealth is never satisfied with his income. This too is meaningless.

Proverbs 31:16-17, 22a, 24, 27; Ecclesiastes 5:10

Week Twenty-Five — Thursday
Money & How It's Different
1 Peter 5:2-3

²Be shepherds of God's flock that is under your care, serving as overseers – not because you must, but because you are willing, as God wants you to be; not greedy for money, but eager to serve; ³not lording it over those entrusted to you, but being examples to the flock.

1 Peter 5:2-3

AS WE GROW TOGETHER

Week Twenty-Five — Friday
House Rules: Decisions: How are they made?
Ephesians 5:17, 23

[17]Therefore do not be foolish, but understand what the Lord's will is. [23]For the husband is the head of the wife as Christ is the head of the church, his body, of which he is the Savior.

Ephesians 5:17, 23

A Prayer Journal for Expectant Couples

Week Twenty-Five — Saturday
House Rules: Answers: who has them?
Ephesians 4:26-27; 5:21

[26]"In your anger do not sin." Do not let the sun go down while you are still angry, [27]and do not give the devil a foothold.
[21]Submit to one another out of reverence for Christ.

Ephesians 4:26-27; 5:21

Week Twenty-Six
Parenthood Has Its Rewards

When you were a child, you and your friends who pretended to be the mom. Your sister could play mommy for hours and you wondered why and how. When pretending to be a parent, she does not count all of the costs or pains or joys. When she pretends to be a great mother, it is a one-sided relationship. The pretend baby doesn't smile unexpectedly or cry for 15 non-stop minutes or have bumps or accidents. Parenting has its rewards and its privileges. Parenthood is a relationship. It is the first relationship that your child experiences. This is your first reward. This baby responds to you and only you until you expose them to others. This relationship with you is the second most important relationship, second only to God. You influence heavily both of those important relationships. How these relationships develop determine how they develop the rest of their relationships, marriage and friendships. Parenting has many rewards, ones you will not experience elsewhere. We will cover God's promises, the gift and responsibility of parenting, and accountability.

One of the rewards that I like the most is the accountability children provide. I dream big. Goals have a date. When I consider what I want for my children, I know that children challenge who you are when you demand their best. I have always wanted my MBA and JD. I want my children to earn a Ph.D. or doctorate of some description. So I am pursuing my MBA, deciding about the JD but will be pursuing a doctorate personally. I want the best for them, so I have to be my best self. Another reward – discovering the best of yourself. A chance to pursue your own dreams to inspire your children to do the same. Parenting is rewarding because it is a clear sign that God trusts you.

Finally, while considering the rewards of parenting, parenting enhances your responsibility. Become more responsible for yourself, your environment and your community and your finances. It is hard to recognize where to enhance your responsibility but examine closely your life because your "microscope" is going to be delivered soon. Your child will be able to see things in your life that you have dismissed. Be responsible.

Sunday	God Keeps His Promises Luke 1:13-18
Monday	Just Enough For You to Handle Matthew 11:28; 1 Peter 5:7

A Prayer Journal for Expectant Couples

Tuesday	The Gift of Child Bearing Luke 1:26-38
Wednesday	Responsibility of Parenting James 1:5
Thursday	Design Your Future (Within God's Will, of course) Proverbs 3:5-6; 16:3-4
Friday	Set A Standard Proverbs 20:11; 22:6
Saturday	Raise The Bar Psalm 139:14; Galatians 5:22-23

As We Grow Together

Week Twenty-Six — Sunday
God Keeps His Promises
Luke 1:13-18

[13]But the angel said to him: "Do not be afraid, Zechariah; your prayer has been heard. Your wife Elizabeth will bear a son, and you are to give him the name John. [18]Zechariah asked the angel, "How can I be sure of this? I am an old man and my wife is well along in years."

Luke 1:13, 18

A PRAYER JOURNAL FOR EXPECTANT COUPLES

Week Twenty-Six — Monday
Just Enough for You to Handle
Matthew 11:28; 1 Peter 5:7

[28]"Come to Me, all you who are weary and burdened, and I will give you rest. [7]Cast <u>all</u> your anxiety on him because he cares for you.

Matthew 11:28; 1 Peter 5:7

AS WE GROW TOGETHER

Week Twenty-Six — Tuesday
The Gift of Child Bearing
Luke 1:26-38

[30]But the angel said to her, "Do not be afraid, Mary, you have found favor with God. [31]You will be with child and give birth to a son, and you are to give him the name Jesus. [34]"How will this be," Mary asked the angel, "Since I am a virgin?" [38]"I am the Lord's servant," Mary answered. "May it be to me as you have said," Then the angel left her.

Luke 1:30, 31, 34, 38

_____
_____
_____
_____
_____
_____
_____
_____
_____
_____
_____
_____
_____
_____
_____
_____
_____
_____
_____
_____
_____
_____
_____
_____

A Prayer Journal for Expectant Couples

Week Twenty-Six — Wednesday
Responsibility of Parenthood
James 1:5

⁵If any of you lacks wisdom, he should ask God, who gives generously to all without finding fault, and it will be given to him.

James 1:5

AS WE GROW TOGETHER

Week Twenty-Six — Thursday
Design Your Future (within God's will, of course)
Proverbs 16:3-4; 3:5-6

³Commit to the Lord whatever you do, and your plans will succeed. ⁴The Lord works out everything for his own ends – even the wicked for a day of disaster. ⁵Trust in the Lord with all your heart and lean not on your own understanding; ⁶in all your ways acknowledge him, and he will make your paths straight.

Proverbs 16:3-4; 3:5-6

A Prayer Journal for Expectant Couples
Week Twenty-Six — Friday
Set A Standard
Proverbs 20:11; 22:6

⁶Train a child in the way he should go and when he is old he will not turn from it. ¹¹Even a child is known by his actions, by whether his conduct is pure and right.

Proverbs 20:11; 22:6

As We Grow Together

Week Twenty-Six — Saturday
Raise the Bar
Psalm 139:14a; Galatians 5:22-23

[14]I praise you because I am fearfully and wonderfully made; [22]But the fruit of the Spirit is love, joy, peace, patience, kindness, goodness, faithfulness, [20]gentleness, and self-control. Against such things there is no law.

Psalm 139:14a; Galatians 5:22-23

A Prayer Journal for Expectant Couples

Week Twenty-Seven
Faith is Required for Parents

In the childbirth preparation class, we did an exercise where we closed our eyes and picked from some cards. On these cards were printed on either side: vaginal/cesarean, no complications/NICU, long labor/short labor, etc. In all of the scenarios, the facilitator explained what to anticipate. Some of the possibilities were horrible but not impossible.

The outcome requires faith.

Our daughter was born at 5 pounds and 7 ounces. The team tried to explain all of the negative possibilities, including feeding her with a tube, and bottle, putting her in NICU, and they were the picture of doom and gloom. I had no problems with the pregnancy, or the birth. She was simply "underweight." I placed that in quotes because while she may have been in an area on the weight chart where they were uncomfortable, God is in control. They threatened me with all kinds of consequences if she didn't gain weight. She needed two ounces. My husband and I prayed over her with our hands on her. God responds to our faith, or lack thereof. Hillary never lost an ounce, gained the two ounces, came home on time and never visited the NICU, tube or bottle feeding.

What do you trust God with?

What are you believing God for?

Our son was born cesarean style. Not what we wanted or expected but truly necessary. The event means nothing once God has shown up. No need for panic or alarm. God's will be done. Submit and surrender. Consider it all joy. Yes, it is easy for me to say.

My niece faced a tragedy after a birth but God is still profoundly awesome. God continued to bless her and she gave birth again triumphantly. God blesses those who believe.

Trust Him with all – it all belongs to Him anyway. Give it all to Him – He knows it all anyway.

Believe that He will handle it all – He is in charge because it is His plans and design.

Sunday   The Faith Quiz: Can you Pass?
                  Hebrews 11:1, 3

As We Grow Together

Monday	Faith: A Commitment to God Hebrews 11:6
Tuesday	Faith: Walk the Walk, Stop Talking Matthew 14:28-31; Luke 8:43-48
Wednesday	Faith: Sometimes Alone Genesis 12-Genesis 22
Thursday	Faith: Pass It On 2 Timothy 1:5-6; Romans 1:12
Friday	Faith: An Action, Not Discussion James 2:26; Matthew 17:20
Saturday	Faith: The Final Word Hebrews 12:2; Matthew 25:21

A PRAYER JOURNAL FOR EXPECTANT COUPLES

Week Twenty-Seven — Sunday
The Faith Quiz: Can You Pass?
Hebrews 11:1, 3

[1]Now faith is being sure of what we hope for and certain of what we do not see. [3]By faith we understand that the universe was formed at God's command, so that what is seen was not made out of what was visible.

Hebrews 11:1, 3

AS WE GROW TOGETHER

Week Twenty-Seven — Monday
Faith: A Commitment to God
Hebrews 11:6

⁶And without faith it is impossible to please God because anyone who comes to him must believe that he exists and that he rewards those who earnestly seek him.

Hebrews 11:6

A Prayer Journal for Expectant Couples

Week Twenty-Seven — Tuesday
Faith: Walk the walk, stop talking
Matthew 14:28-31; Luke 8:43-48

^{31}Immediately Jesus reached out his hand and caught him. "You of little faith," he said, "why did you doubt?"
^{47}Then the woman, seeing that she could not go unnoticed, came trembling and fell at his feet. In the presence of all the people, she told why she had touched him and how she had been instantly healed. ^{48}Then he said to her, "Daughter, your faith has healed you. Go in peace."

Matthew 14:31; Luke 8:47-48

_____
_____
_____
_____
_____
_____
_____
_____
_____
_____
_____
_____
_____
_____
_____
_____
_____
_____
_____
_____

As We Grow Together

Week Twenty-Seven — Wednesday
Faith: Sometimes Alone
Genesis 12 - Genesis 22

[1]The Lord had said to Abraham, "Leave your country, your people and your father's household and go to the land I will show you.

Genesis 12:1

A Prayer Journal for Expectant Couples
Week Twenty-Seven — Thursday
Faith: Pass It On
2 Timothy 1:5-6; Romans 1:12

⁵I have been reminded of your sincere faith, which first lived in your grandmother Loris and your mother Eunice and, I am persuaded, now live in you also. ⁶For this reason I remind you to fan into flame the gift of God, which is in you through laying on of my hands. ¹²That is, that you and I may be mutually encouraged by each other's faith.

2 Timothy 1:5-6; Romans 1:12

AS WE GROW TOGETHER

Week Twenty-Seven — Friday
Faith: An Action, Not Discussion
James 2:26; Matthew 17:20

[26]As the body without the spirit is dead, so faith without deeds is dead. [20]He replied, "Because you have so little faith. I tell you the truth, if you have faith as small as a mustard seed, you can say to this mountain, 'Move from here to there' and it will move. Nothing will be impossible for you."

James 2:26; Matthew 17:20

_____
_____
_____
_____
_____
_____
_____
_____
_____
_____
_____
_____
_____
_____
_____
_____
_____
_____
_____
_____
_____
_____

A Prayer Journal for Expectant Couples
Week Twenty-Seven — Saturday
Faith: The Final Word
Hebrews 12:2; Matthew 25:21

[2]Let us fix our eyes on Jesus, the author and perfecter of our faith, who for the joy set before him endured the cross, scorning its shame, and sat down at the right hand of the throne of God. [21]"His master replied 'Well done, good and faithful servant! You have been faithful with a few things. Come and share your master's happiness!'"

Hebrews 12:2; Matthew 25:21

Week Twenty-Eight
The Lessons Ahead

Your child also has the job of teaching you lessons. There are many lessons you have ahead. For those of you who may miss the lessons on the first round, there is great news. The lessons are presented until we get it. I promise. These lessons are for both of you. The lessons also expose your character traits and sharpens them. When this happens consider that education that is for you now, will later be used for them as well. God wastes nothing. God does not waste any opportunities for his glory to shine as well as for us to learn more ways to praise and glorify Him these lessons.

Lessons are multi-dimensional. These are the lessons we learn to move us forward. These are lessons we learn so we become closer to God. Then, these are lessons we learn so that we can reprioritize our lives. In all of these, the lessons are not new, but function as a reminder of how God really designed life.

Children do not possess fear. We teach fear based on our actions. Or lack of action. When we learn from their fearlessness, we learn to move forward and release our fears. Further, we learn to stop preventing them from moving forward. We also learn to stop teaching fear and start teaching abundant thinking and living. Finally, we are reunited with God's teaching of casting our fears on Him.

Next, there are the lessons which bring us closer to God and reestablishes accountability. As they grow older, they hold you accountable for your activities. We have a list of words that are off-limits. When my daughter hears me say one of them, she immediately says that she will tell my mother, and that I know better. When the five year old in your life challenges your obedience to your rules, she reminds you that you are the parent and she is expecting your best. Her accountability also reminds you that you are accountable to God. Your parental relationship brings you closer to God.

Another lesson is remembering to dream, set big goals, and work hard.

Lastly, God wants us to leave our fears with Him. You must teach that to your child. In order to do that, you have to live that command.

You can only teach what you live.

Sunday	Show her your prayer life early
	2 Chronicles 7:14; Luke 6:28; 1 Thessalonians

A Prayer Journal for Expectant Couples

	5:17; Matthew 5:44, 6:5
Monday	Document his many firsts Ecclesiastes 3:1-8
Tuesday	Hug her as often as possible Matthew 3:17
Wednesday	Make every moment count – each one is important Ecclesiastes 3:11-14
Thursday	Your marriage still requires the same attention Ephesians 5; 1 Peter 3:1-7
Friday	I rarely remember the disadvantages or hard times 1 Corinthians 13:5; Matthew 18:21-22
Saturday	Your career and family sometimes conflict Genesis 1:26; 2:18; Proverbs 31:10-31

As We Grow Together

Week Twenty-Eight — Sunday
Show her your prayer life early
2 Chronicles 7:14; Matthew 5:44, 6:5-13; Luke 6:28;
1 Thessalonians 5:17

[14]if my people, who are called by my name, will humble themselves and pray and seek my face and turn from their wicked ways, then will I hear from heaven and will forgive their sin and will heal their land.

[44]But I tell you: Love your enemies and pray for those who persecute you.

[28]bless those who curse you, pray for those who mistreat you

[17]pray continually

2 Chronicles 7:14; Matthew 5:44; Luke 6:28; 1 Thessalonians 5:17

A Prayer Journal for Expectant Couples

Week Twenty-Eight — Monday
Document his many firsts. Record all you can as many ways you can
Ecclesiastes 3:2

[2]A time to be born and a time to die.

Ecclesiastes 3:2

AS WE GROW TOGETHER

Week Twenty-Eight — Tuesday
Hug her as often as possible
Matthew 3:17

[17]And a voice from heaven said, "This is my Son, whom I love; with him I am well pleased."

Matthew 3:17

A Prayer Journal for Expectant Couples

Week Twenty-Eight — Wednesday
Make every moment count – each one is important
Ecclesiastes 3:11-14

[12]I know that there is nothing better for men than to be happy and do good while they live.

Ecclesiastes 3:12

As We Grow Together

Week Twenty-Eight — Thursday
Your marriage still requires the same attention
1 Peter 3:1-7; Ephesians 5

[7]Husbands, in the same way be considerate as you live with your wives, and treat them with respect as the weaker partner and as heirs with you of the gracious gift of life, so that nothing will hinder your prayers.

1 Peter 3:7

A Prayer Journal for Expectant Couples

Week Twenty-Eight — Friday
Your Grudge is Your Anchor
(I rarely remember the disadvantages or hard times)
Matthew 18:21-22; 1 Corinthians 13:5

[21] Then Peter came to Jesus and asked, "Lord, how many times shall I forgive my brother when he sins against me? Up to seven times?
[22] Jesus answered, "I tell you, not seven times, but seventy-seven times.
[5] (It) love keeps no record of wrongs."

Matthew 18:21-22; 1 Corinthians 13:5

AS WE GROW TOGETHER

Week Twenty-Eight — Saturday
Your career and family sometimes conflict.
You may challenge your decision to return to work
Genesis 1:26, 2:18; Proverbs 31:10-31

²⁶Then God said, "Let us make man in our image, in our likeness, and let them rule over the fish of the sea and the birds of the air, over the livestock, over all the earth, and over all the creatures that move along the ground." ¹⁸The Lord God said, "It is not good for man to be alone. I will make a helper suitable for him."

Genesis 1:26, 2:18

Week Twenty-Nine
Life is Short – Do What Matters

Life is too short for worry, anxiety, anger, bitterness and grudges. I was pregnant on September 11, 2001. I was at home, going to work later but not really feeling great. I watched the tragedy happen. 2002 brought the one year anniversary of the day our national security was breached. I watched the special hosted by Diane Sawyer about the 65 children born of the September 11 tragedy.

Each day 63 women are reminded of the day which changed their entire lives. Best scenario: They were all at peace. They were perfectly happy. Worst scenario: They were unhappy. They had just had a fight. The fact is they were never able to make it right. Don't fall victim to that – make it right always.

When you consider your marriage and any issues, contemplate whether they are serious enough to hold on to. Ask yourself will it matter in twenty minutes. When you consider life's overall impact on you life, then some of the issues that really bother you may not be that important.

Life is too short. Do what matters. Decide what's important. Family time is ultimately important. What time is allocated to family? Are your dinners family style where everyone is at the same table and there is no television? This is true family time. How do you spend your weekends? Are your weekends dedicated to growing closer as a family? Do you take time to listen to the children? Can you modify your hours at work so that the family can eat dinner together?

There were several thousand stories from the survivors of 9/11. There is one that touches my heart the most. The owner of a company who was on floor 104 one away from the top, was walking his child to school the morning of the tragedy. His child asked him to walk her to school that morning. He agreed reluctantly because he would be late to work. He agreed and walked the child. He arrived at the area after the explosions. If he had been on time, if he had not walked the child to school, he would not be alive. It doesn't matter who he was, what he owned, the gender of the child, however, it does matter that he did what was important. We have 18 short years before they are no longer children. We need to make the most of each of those days.

What are you going to do to make the moments count and matter?

AS WE GROW TOGETHER

Sunday	Prayer is Power Romans 8:26
Monday	Love John 3:16
Tuesday	Timing Is Everything (Quality Time) Ecclesiastes 3:7-8a
Wednesday	Listening is a Skill James 1:19
Thursday	Quiet Time Psalm 1:2; 19:14; 145:5
Friday	Conflict Resolution is Essential Ephesians 4:26-27; Proverbs 15:1, 18; 17:9, 14
Saturday	Family Philosophy Joshua 22:5

A Prayer Journal for Expectant Couples
Week Twenty-Nine — Sunday
Prayer is Power
Romans 8:26

[26]In the same way, the Spirit helps us in our weakness. We do not know what we ought to pray for, but the Spirit himself intercedes for us with groans that words cannot express.

Romans 8:26

Week Twenty-Nine — Monday
Love
John 3:16

[16]For God so loved the world that He gave His only begotten son that whosoever believes in Him should not perish but have everlasting life.

John 3:16

_____
_____
_____
_____
_____
_____
_____
_____
_____
_____
_____
_____
_____
_____
_____
_____
_____
_____
_____
_____
_____
_____
_____
_____
_____
_____
_____
_____

A Prayer Journal for Expectant Couples

Week Twenty-Nine — Tuesday
Timing is Everything
Ecclesiastes 3:7b-8a

[7b]a time to be silent and a time to speak, [8a]a time to love and a time to hate.

Ecclesiastes 3:7b-8a

AS WE GROW TOGETHER

Week Twenty-Nine — Wednesday
Listening is a Skill
James 1:19

[19]My dear brothers, take note of this: Everyone should be quick to listen, slow to speak and slow to become angry,

James 1:19

A Prayer Journal for Expectant Couples

Week Twenty-Nine — Thursday
Quiet Time
Psalm 1:2; 19:14; 145:5

²But his delight is in the law of the Lord, and on his law he meditates day and night. ¹⁴May the words of my mouth and the meditation of my heart be pleasing in your sight, O Lord, my Rock and my Redeemer. ⁵They will speak of the glorious splendor of the majesty, and I will meditate on your wonderful works.

Psalm 1:2; 19:14; 145:5

AS WE GROW TOGETHER
Week Twenty-Nine — Friday
Conflict Resolution is Essential
Ephesians 4:26-27; Proverbs 15:1, 18, 17:9, 14

[26]"In your anger, do not sin. Do not let the sun go down while you are still angry, [27]and do not give the devil a foothold."
[1]A gentle answer turns away wrath, but a harsh word stirs up anger.
[18]A hot-tempered man stirs up dissension, but a patient man calms a quarrel.
[9]He who covers over an offense promotes love, but whoever repeats the matter separates close friends. [14]Starting a quarrel is like breaching a dam; so drop the matter before a dispute breaks out.
Ephesians 4:26-27; Proverbs 15:1, 18, 17:9, 14

A Prayer Journal for Expectant Couples

Week Twenty-Nine — Saturday
Family Philosophy
Joshua 22:5

²²"But be very careful to keep the commandment and the law that Moses the servant of the Lord gave you: to love the Lord your God, to walk in all his ways, to obey his commands, to hold fast to him and to serve him with all your heart and all your soul."

Joshua 22:5

Week Thirty
In Ten Weeks

In ten short weeks, you will be a parent. Excitement and fear may have anchored themselves within you. You may be exhausted and also tired of people asking when you are due, what you are having, what you will name that person and rubbing your stomach.

In ten short weeks, you will experience sleepless nights, odd hours, cold meals, pure exhaustion, and a new person. This new person comes equipped with her own personality and temperament and love. This person, this baby, will steal your heart even before you hold him. Absolutely promise. In the next ten weeks, you have work to do, though. Dreaming has to be allocated. This time will pass quickly.

As you prepare for the arrival, a birthing preparation class assists you in knowing what to anticipate. During the class, after you exercise your breathing, they share valuable information about pain medication options and the side effects and any associated risks. Also, they share the other possible outcomes, particularly changes in the birth plan. When I had Hillary, I didn't have pain medication and gave birth naturally. When I had Nehemiah, I had to have a cesarean section and pain medication was required. The surgery wasn't optional.

Consider over the next several weeks how your lifestyle will change. Do you need a housekeeper? Who will help you after your husband returns to work? What is the family plan? Now is when those discussions are important. Eat as many hot meals as possible and enjoy the lack of interruption. Decorate the nursery. Prepare for the bundle with the energy you have.

Remember to relax and respond to your body's needs. You have a lifetime ahead. This is an exciting time and you want to remember this time as exciting.

Names are important. Carefully select his name. He has to use it his whole life. I don't like nicknames so I expect his name to be used without modifications or changes. Lastly, it needs to mean something and be respected. His name attaches him to his family.

Sunday	The Arrival
Monday	A Room of Her Own
Tuesday	Names Are a Legacy

A Prayer Journal for Expectant Couples

Wednesday   Care for Your Child

Thursday   Your Revised Lifestyle

Friday   Your Thoughts are Important

Saturday   Your Feelings are Important, too

AS WE GROW TOGETHER

Week Thirty — Sunday
The Arrival

What is the plan? What is the backup plan? What is the third option? What happens when all plans fail?

A Prayer Journal for Expectant Couples

Week Thirty — Monday
A Room of Her Own

What will the nursery look like? What theme? What kind of crib? Will you want a chair in the nursery? Details. Details. Details.

As We Grow Together

Week Thirty — Tuesday
Names are a Legacy

Is that a family name?
How did you get your name?
What is the origin of your name?
What does your name mean?
How do you spell that?
Can you repeat your name?
Do you know _____ (someone with same name)?
Are you related to _____?
Are you _____ little sister/brother/daughter/son?

___
___
___
___
___
___
___
___
___
___
___
___
___
___
___
___
___
___
___
___
___
___

A Prayer Journal for Expectant Couples

Week Thirty — Wednesday
Care for Your Child

Decisions for the rest of his life are being made as your eyes cross this page by you and many others who don't even know your child, such as governmental officials.

As We Grow Together

Week Thirty — Thursday
Your Revised Lifestyle

No, you can't just do what you feel like doing. No, your meals will be different. No, you don't go to the bathroom alone anymore. No, all of your money is no longer yours anymore.

_____
_____
_____
_____
_____
_____
_____
_____
_____
_____
_____
_____
_____
_____
_____
_____
_____
_____
_____
_____
_____
_____
_____
_____
_____

A Prayer Journal for Expectant Couples
Week Thirty — Friday
Your Thoughts are Important

Your thoughts are important to God, your spouse, your family, your friends and people who care about you. Your thoughts need to be shared and your impact into decisions and conversations is very important.

_____
_____
_____
_____
_____
_____
_____
_____
_____
_____
_____
_____
_____
_____
_____
_____
_____
_____
_____
_____
_____
_____
_____
_____
_____
_____

As We Grow Together

Week Thirty — Saturday
Your Feelings are Important, Too

Similar to your thoughts, your feelings are important, maybe even more so than your thoughts. Your feelings drive your thoughts. Be prepared to be honest about your feelings with yourself, your spouse, your friends, family and others.

_____
_____
_____
_____
_____
_____
_____
_____
_____
_____
_____
_____
_____
_____
_____
_____
_____
_____
_____
_____
_____
_____
_____
_____
_____

A Prayer Journal for Expectant Couples

Week Thirty-One
Birth & Its Complexities

Twenty-five weeks ago, you were celebrating and excited. Now you may still be excited but you are not addressing the actual arrival. Childbirth is a daily occurrence around the globe, whether in the plush hospital in Houston, Texas or on the red clay in a hut in a third world country. You are not likely to create any milestones but your birth experience will be special.

It is about now that you have considered a birth plan. You have heard that birth involves pain. You are sure that you want to avoid that, but I am certain that there is not a way to avoid that pain. I wish there was a way.

Now we have to deal with reality. What is the plan to handle the pain? Do you and your spouse agree? Will you need a backup plan?

During this week we will also talk about the history of childbirth pains. Birth is complex and the pain that it produces is also complex. If you haven't already gone to the class, then when you go you will contemplate several scenarios. One of those scenarios is pain medication versus none. Pain medication usually refers to the epidural, where you are administered an injection in your back near your spine. As a result you don't feel anything from the waist down until several hours later. Other medicines are administered differently and are used in different situations.

The backup plan is for when your situation changes and a different medicine may be required rather than optional. You also want to consider your pain threshold and the possible side effects. You may want to consult your physician, do some internet research and ask your friends and co-workers what their family did about pain. Everyone deals with this and each woman may have more than one story based on the number of children she has.

Consider the following pages carefully. You are deciding on something that affects your experiences. I thought that my experiences were going to be same with both children but I was wrong. They were as different as night and day. I will never forget them nor do I regret them. I cannot possibly figure how the experience could've been different.

Sunday	Eve and the Sentence We Endure Genesis
Monday	Is Redemption Possible? Eve's Reaction to God's Sentence Genesis
Tuesday	The List They Give You at the Hospital
Wednesday	Pain Medication: The Game Plan
Thursday	My Personal Choice & Testimony for Child One
Friday	My Personal Choice & Testimony for Child Two
Saturday	What is Best for the Baby

A Prayer Journal for Expectant Couples

Week Thirty-One — Sunday
Eve and the Sentence We Endure
Genesis

Eve sinned. She disobeyed God. She was the first one to sin. Because of her sin, we were promised pain during childbirth. Eve was created in the image of God from one of Adam's ribs. He created Eve as a companion and helpmate for Adam. Adam was in charge of Eve and the whole Earth and everything in it.

As We Grow Together
Week Thirty-One — Monday
Is Redemption Possible? Eve's Reaction to God's Sentence
Genesis

Yes, Eve did. Yes, we also are disciplined for Eve's transgression. Can we ask for forgiveness for Eve and be relieved from this consequence? Sure we could ask but why would God do that now?

A Prayer Journal for Expectant Couples

Week Thirty-One — Tuesday
The List They Give You at the Hospital

In short, the list is based on experience. Use this information to your advantage. If you don't understand how something could be instrumental in childbirth, ask. They will help you. Keep this list close to you in case you need to reference it for the next child as well.

As We Grow Together

Week Thirty-One — Wednesday
Pain Medication: The Game Plan

We spoke earlier about pain medication options. There are several options to consider. One is Demerol. This is a mild pain reliever. There are others along this same line. The next level up is the epidural. When pain medication is offered this is usually what is being referred to. This medication requires an anesthesiologist.

Don't be afraid to share you concerns with your doctor. They need to know so that you are in total agreement about what is expected and desired.

A Prayer Journal for Expectant Couples

Week Thirty-One — Thursday
My Personal Choice & Testimony for Child One

In the class I always refer to, I decided to have my child by natural methods meaning: NO PAIN MEDICATION! Yes, read those words again. I had heard the concerns about the aftereffects of the medicine on the mother and the child. In addition, I had to decide that I was up for the challenge. I had to decide how much pain I could tolerate. I went for natural.

_____
_____
_____
_____
_____
_____
_____
_____
_____
_____
_____
_____
_____
_____
_____
_____
_____
_____
_____
_____
_____
_____
_____

As We Grow Together

Week Thirty-One — Friday
My Personal Choice & Testimony for Child Two

The second birth was quite far from my wildest dreams and certainly my imagination. Again I reflected on my daughter's birth and said I would do it all again the same way. I packed that entire bag. This time I didn't use a single item, well maybe a few things.

A Prayer Journal for Expectant Couples

Week Thirty-One — Saturday
What is Best for the Baby

The bottom line is what is best for the baby is the <u>most</u> important person to consider. Your health is equally important but that baby is inside and we can't see if she is okay or if the umbilical cord is cutting off the circulation to some part of the body. That baby can't knock on your uterus and say help. Time is of the essence when a baby is in distress.

Week Thirty-Two
Biblical Parents

God created and ordained parenting. God gives directives to parents about what to do, what to name, how and when to discipline and when you will be blessed with children. God chooses parents. God promised certain blessings, some are in the form of children. God gifts you to parent. God gives us the lives of several parents, whose lives have changed as parents. They are not perfect, even though they are Biblical. As parents, we all have our trials and triumphs. These parents lead the way with lessons about God's expectations. You may find yourself in these examples or someone you know. Realizing that parenthood is God ordained, and knowing that God communicated directly with these parents, there were still some obedience issues.

We are the same parents that they are: anxious, impatient, strategic and victorious. Simultaneously. Parents are driven by successful events. Those events range from successful births to academics to spiritual leadership. By Broussard's definition, success is a result of being in God's will. In other words, He allowed this event to be successful so this was His will. While this may not stand the absolute test of time, I do have substantial evidence supporting my claim.

Parents make mistakes and miracles on a daily basis. When you error, forgive yourself, apologize and move forward. Do not wallow in either miracle or mistake. You cannot afford to spend time basking because you will miss the defense at the other end of the court, a basketball analogy. What happens is that we will miss some details if we are focusing that last outcome.

Be a PARENT. There are some people who have children who do not parent. Be strong, decisive, meek and humble. Parenting is hard work and requires perseverance and patience and engagement. Successful parents rely on God's wisdom, strength, guidance and His word.

Last note on parenting. Parenting is a full-time, round the clock, thankless, researching job that pays in huge smiles, laughter, colds, and love. Parenting does not stop when they leave home. Parenting stops when one of you dies, not before. Keep parenting.

Sunday	The Parent Who Laughs Genesis 21:1-7
Monday	Parent With Faith Genesis 22:1-19

A Prayer Journal for Expectant Couples

Tuesday	Parenting With God's Favor Genesis 17:5-6
Wednesday	Parent With Trust Genesis 9:1, 8, 11
Thursday	Parent as Protector Genesis 21:11
Friday	Parenting Requires Resourcefulness 1 Kings 17:12-16; Matthew 14:13-21
Saturday	Parenting With Love John 3:16

AS WE GROW TOGETHER

Week Thirty-Two — Sunday
The Parent who Laughs
Genesis 21:1-7

⁶Sarah said, "God has brought me laughter, and everyone who hears about this will laugh with me."

Genesis 21:6

A PRAYER JOURNAL FOR EXPECTANT COUPLES

Week Thirty-Two — Monday
Parents with Faith
Genesis 22:1-19

¹Some time later God tested Abraham. He said to him, "Abraham." "Here I am," he replied. ²Then God said, "Take your son, your only son, Isaac, whom you love, and go to the region of Moriah. Sacrifice him there as a burnt offering on one of the mountains I will tell you about."

Genesis 22:1-2

AS WE GROW TOGETHER

Week Thirty-Two — Tuesday
Parenting with God's Favor
Genesis 17:5-6

⁵No longer will you be called Abram; your name will be Abraham for I have made you a father of many nations. ⁶I will make you fruitful; I will make nations of you, and kings will come from you.

Genesis 17:5-6

A Prayer Journal for Expectant Couples

Week Thirty-Two — Wednesday
Parent with Trust
Genesis 9:1, 8, 11

[1]Then God blessed Noah and his sons, saying to them, "Be fruitful and increase in number and fill the earth." [8]Then God said to Noah and to his sons with him: "I establish my covenant with you: Never again will all life be cut off by the waters of a flood; never again will there be a flood to destroy the Earth."

Genesis 9:1, 8

AS WE GROW TOGETHER

Week Thirty-Two — Thursday
Parent as Protector
Genesis 21:11

[11] The matter distressed Abraham greatly because it concerned his son.
Genesis 21:11

A Prayer Journal for Expectant Couples

Week Thirty-Two — Friday
Parenting Requires Resourcefulness
1 Kings 17:12-16; Matthew 14:13-21

[14]For this is what the Lord, the God of Israel, says: 'the jar of flour will not be used and the jug of oil will not run dry until the day the Lord gives rain on the land.' [20]They all ate and were satisfied, and the disciples picked up twelve basketfuls of broken pieces that were left over.

1 Kings 17:14; Matthew 14:20

AS WE GROW TOGETHER

Week Thirty-Two — Saturday
Parenting with Love
John 3:16

[16] "For God so loved the world that He gave His one and only son, that whoever believes in Him shall not perish but have eternal life."

John 3:16

A Prayer Journal for Expectant Couples

Week Thirty-Three
Biblical Parents

The hardest job you'll ever have is and it is also the most rewarding of all the jobs you'll ever have. God created parenting, all of the expectations of parenting, along with the responsibilities, rewards, privileges, pains, and sacrifices. God ordained parenthood and continues to instruct parents on how to do what He gifts us to do. God empowers us to parent through His extraordinary omnipresence, grace and forgiveness. Biblical parents make mistakes, too, and great sacrifices. Also, Biblical parents have access to the Lord's guidance and submit to His leadership. We have hardships as parents but we have victories and miracles. The book of Genesis provides countless examples of parenthood, some for us to follow and some for us to avoid. The lessons presented and learned in parenting are both subtle and obvious.

When you see your child for the very first time, you have then truly experienced God's touch and His warm embrace. I could hear His voice so much clearer when I had my daughter and He really showed up and out when I birthed my son.

Biblical parents lead their families the way God requests. Biblical parents learn and grow spiritually as parents from God, mentor parents, their children and their triumphs and mistakes.

Biblical parents seek mentorship from other Biblical parents. Biblical parents pray for their children and are committed to their spiritual growth and relationship. When I studied Catholicism, I discovered that the religion requires the parent to raise their child as a Catholic. While this may be an unspoken rule in other faiths, in Catholicism this is a rule that if not followed, there may be judgement for the parents. The point is that as Biblical parents, there should be certain commitments, practices and guidelines that we need to follow and implement in our homes and as a part of our parenting.

Biblical parenting also has standards. There is an additional level of accountability because we have access to God who has gifted us to be parents and the tools He provides. God expects us to be Biblical parents. When we have problems, we seek Him.

Sunday	Parenting as a Student Deuteronomy 4:9; Proverbs 22:6
Monday	Parenting with Conviction

As We Grow Together

Psalm 51:10

Tuesday	Parenting with Commitment 1 Kings 8:61; 2 Chronicles 16:9a
Wednesday	Parenting with Wisdom Proverbs 31:26; Psalm 111:10; James 1:5
Thursday	Parenting with Pride Genesis 21:8
Friday	Parenting with Leadership Proverbs 23:13; Isaiah 11:6
Saturday	Parenting with a Legacy Genesis 17:6; Deuteronomy 4:9

A PRAYER JOURNAL FOR EXPECTANT COUPLES

Week Thirty-Three — Sunday
Parenting as a Student
Deuteronomy 4:9; Proverbs 22:6

⁹Only be careful, and watch yourselves closely so that you do not forget the things your eyes have seen or let them slip from your heart as long as you live. Teach them to your children and to their children after them. ⁶Train up a child in the way he should go, and when he is old he will not turn from it.

Deuteronomy 4:9; Proverbs 22:6

_____
_____
_____
_____
_____
_____
_____
_____
_____
_____
_____
_____
_____
_____
_____
_____
_____
_____
_____
_____
_____
_____
_____
_____

As We Grow Together

Week Thirty-Three — Monday
Parenting with Conviction
Psalm 51:10

[10]Create in me a pure heart, O God, and renew a steadfast spirit within me.

Psalm 51:10

A Prayer Journal for Expectant Couples

Week Thirty-Three — Tuesday
Parenting with Commitment
1 Kings 8:61; 2 Chronicles 16:9a

⁶¹But your hearts must be fully committed to the Lord our God, to live by His decrees and obey His commands, at this time. ᵃFor the eyes of the Lord, range throughout the earth to strengthen those whose hearts are fully committed to Him.

1 Kings 8:61; 2 Chronicles 16:9a

As We Grow Together

Week Thirty-Three — Wednesday
Parenting with Wisdom
Proverbs 31:26; Psalm 111:10; James 1:5

²⁶She speaks with wisdom, and faithful instruction is on her tongue.
¹⁰The fear of the Lord is the beginning of wisdom;
⁵If any of you lacks wisdom, he should ask God, who gives generously to all without finding fault, and it will be given to him.

Proverbs 31:26; Psalm 111:10; James 1:5

A Prayer Journal for Expectant Couples

Week Thirty-Three — Thursday
Parenting with Pride
Genesis 21:8

[8] The child grew and was weaned, and on the day Isaac was weaned, Abraham held a great feast.

Genesis 21:8

As We Grow Together

Week Thirty-Three — Friday
Parenting with Leadership
Proverbs 23:13; Isaiah 11:6

[13]Do not withhold discipline from a child if you punish him with the rod, he will not die. [6b]and a little child will lead them.

Proverbs 23:13; Isaiah 11:6

A Prayer Journal for Expectant Couples

Week Thirty-Three — Saturday
Parenting with a Legacy
Genesis 17:6; Deuteronomy 4:9

⁶I will make you very fruitful; I will make nations of you, and kings will come from you.

Genesis 17:6

Week Thirty Four
Complex Family Discrepancies

Every family has complexities. We all have family members we are not proud of. For all applicable reasons, all family members do not get along. Families are complex entities. Members have their favorite members. The family history is sometimes sordid and often members are not completely clear about what happened at all. The Bible seems to be no different. We will discuss some families who are true leaders among their peers, but have some family issues.

Our purpose of covering them and their issues is to discuss how you and your spouse handle family issues. We are also going to investigate how certain situations could be different. We will discuss family secrets and family lies.

As the matriarch and patriarch, this is the time to break old, bad habits and create new traditions. At the same time, you can decide how family issues are handled rather than resort to the lies and the cover up. Family discrepancies are the foundation for who your child will become and how your child will handle life issues and conflict.

As we investigate the families of Abraham and Sarah, Isaac and Rebekah, Jacob, Leah and Rachel, Noah and his sons, Abraham and Keturah, and Abraham and Haggar, we will consider what they did right, wrong and how to apply these principles to our families.

Generational curses also exist and it is our job to end these curses and patterns through examples and prayer. Communication and forgiveness are keys to ending generational curses and patterns. Honesty plays a role; however, families tend not to be honest.

The most embarrassing event as an adult is being told you have additional family members and you find out from a stranger. Then when said adult asks or confronts her family she receives less than the anticipated truth from her family. The family acts as if they would never have to face these issues. The family stills try to work around the truth. Make a pact with you spouse and family to tell the truth and reveal the family secrets. Figure out how to get past the generational curses. The enemy wishes the secrets remain secrets. When the truth is revealed, the family thrives.

Sunday: Banishing Anxiety
Genesis 16

A Prayer Journal for Expectant Couples

Monday:	God's Promises Are Real Genesis 17:19; 21:1-3
Tuesday:	The Promise is Fulfilled Genesis 24:4
Wednesday:	Family Traditions Enforced/A Breach of Trust Genesis 29:26-27
Thursday:	A Man of Honor Genesis 29: 28-30; 29:11
Friday:	Blended Families Genesis 25:1-11
Saturday:	Then He Trusts You & The Children He Gifts Genesis 6, 7, 8, & 9; Genesis 6: 7-8, 14-18

Week Thirty-Four — Sunday
Anxiety Birthed Ishmael/Banishing Anxiety
Genesis 16

Lack of faith + your time = anxiety. Sarah used this equation to introduce anxiety in her own family history and legacy. She was in a hurry for a child defined as God's blessings. We could put our name in the blank on issues, maybe not that exact issue. I introduced anxiety about my daughter's education. The biggest mistake we make is that we want what we want when we want it. Our time is not Gods time. Because He has the master plan and He knows the outcome of our mistakes and anxieties. He is in charge of the timing of all that we experience.

A Prayer Journal for Expectant Couples

Week Thirty-Four — Monday
God Promised Isaac — God Promises Are Real
Genesis 17: 19; 21: 1-3

¹Now the Lord was gracious to Sarah as he had said, and the Lord did for Sarah what he had promised. ²Sarah became pregnant and bore a son to Abraham in his old age, at the very time God had promised him. ³Abraham gave the name Isaac to the son Sarah bore him.

Genesis 21:1-3

Week Thirty-Four — Tuesday
The Promise is Fulfilled
Genesis 24:4

⁴but will go to my country and my own relatives and get a wife for my son Isaac.

Genesis 24:4

A Prayer Journal for Expectant Couples

Week Thirty-Four — Wednesday
Family Traditions Enforced
Genesis 29:26-27

²⁶Laban replied, "It is not our custom here to give the younger daughter in marriage before the older one. ²⁷Finish this daughter's Bridal week; then we will give you the younger one also, in return for another seven years of work."

Genesis 29:26-27

Week Thirty-Four — Thursday
A Man of Honor
Genesis 29:11, 28-30

¹¹Then Jacob kissed Rachel and began to weep aloud. ²⁸And Jacob did so. He finished the week with Leah, and then Laban gave him his daughter Rachel to be his wife. ²⁹Laban gave his servant girl Bilhah to his daughter Rachel as her maidservant. ³⁰Jacob lay with Rachel also, and he loved Rachel more than Leah. And he worked for Laban another seven years.

Genesis 29:11, 28-30

A Prayer Journal for Expectant Couples

Week Thirty-Four — Friday
(With No Strings Attached) Blended Families
Genesis 25: 1-11

¹Abraham took another wife, whose name was Keturah. ²She bore him Zimran, Joksan, Medan, Midian, Ishbak, and Shuah. ³Jokshan was the father of Dedan; the descendants of Dedan were the Asshurities, the Letushities and the Leummites. ⁴The sons of Midian were Ephan, Epher, Hanoch, Abida and Eldaah. All these were descendants of Keturah. ⁵Abraham left everything he owned to Isaac. ⁶But when he was still living, he gave gifts to the sons of his concubines and sent them away from his son Isaac to the land of the east. ⁷Altogether, Abraham lived a hundred and seventy-five years. ⁸Then Abraham breathed his last and dies at a good old age, an old man and full of years; and he was gathered to his people. ⁹His sons Isaac and Ishmeal buried him in the cave of Machpelah near Mamre, in the field of Ephron of Zohar the Hittite, ¹⁰the field Abraham had bought from Hittities. There Abraham was buried with his wife Sarah. ¹¹After Abraham's death, God blessed his son Isaac, who then lived near Beer Luhai Roi.

Genesis 25: 1-11

AS WE GROW TOGETHER

Week Thirty-Four — Saturday
When He Trusts You and The Children He Gifts
Genesis 9: 1, 8, 11

¹Then God blessed Noah and his sons, saying to them, "Be fruitful and increase in number and fill the earth. ⁸Then God said to Noah and to his sons with him. ¹¹I establish my covenant with you: Never again will all life be cut off by the waters of a flood; never again will there be a flood to destroy the earth.

Genesis 9: 1, 8, 11

Week Thirty-Five
Children of the Bible

When you read about children, your reality is surreal. Each person came from a woman – a parent. As a parent, we cannot possibly imagine or plan all the things that your child will see, accomplish or achieve in their lifetime. You have no idea if your child will be the 55th President of the United States or a teacher or travel with Cirque de Soliel. Our children are exceptional creatures who are blessed by God based on what He has planned for them as well as how He blessed them based on the promises He has made to us as parents. Similar to the covenant God made with Abraham, God has a covenant with us as parents.

The children of the Bible we will discuss this week are extraordinary and resilient and unbelievable. These children are exactly how our children are. Our children are extraordinary who are made by God and will do what He says, and no, it won't make since to you sometimes. Our children are resilient. They rise above the "stuff" which sinks us and stifles us and stalls us and stops us. They don't respond like us. They do not quit. They are creative when seeking solutions. Our children are unbelievable. They do things we won't do and sometimes hoped that they would never do. They do what they want to do. They do the socially questionable. They are inquisitive. They are thoughtful. They believe. They have faith. They are our children.

Children teach us life lessons. They teach us those lessons we have forgotten, ignored, avoided, and missed. They remind us to live breath, and laugh. They teach us to laugh at ourselves, to clap at the really important time – times that happen daily. They remind us to live in the moment.

Children are a mirror of us, if only we had the courage to do what we are truly called to do.

AS WE GROW TOGETHER

We will discuss Joseph, his brothers, Cain, Able, Ruth, the Prodigal Son, his brother, and his father and how to parent these children. We are encouraged by their stories to remain focused as parents, to continue to seek God's face for our lives and our children's lives, to remember we are stewards of their lives – God is really the author of their stories. We are their Earthly guidance. God is their heavenly Father.

Sunday:	The Whole Story Revealed: Joseph Chosen Genesis 37: 28, 36; 45: 3-9
Monday:	If You Could, Would You Change Your Mind? Genesis 37: 3-5, 8, 11, 31-36
Tuesday:	Jealousy to the Highest Power Genesis 4: 1-16
Wednesday:	Where You Go, I will Go Ruth
Thursday:	A Model Father: A True Role Model Luke 15: 11, 20b, 22-24, 31-32
Friday:	Wisdom Develops Over Time Luke 15: 12-20a, 21
Saturday:	Can't See the Forest Because of the Trees Luke 15: 2-30

A PRAYER JOURNAL FOR EXPECTANT COUPLES

Week Thirty-Five — Sunday
The Whole Story Revealed: Joseph Chosen
Genesis 37:3, 36; 45: 3-9

³Now Israel loved Joseph more than any of his other sons, because he had been born to him in his old age; and he made a richly ornamented robe for him. ³⁶Meanwhile, the Midianites sold Joseph in Egypt to Potiphar, one of Pharaoh's officials, the captain of the guard. ³Joseph said to his brothers, "I am Joseph! Is my father still living?" But his brothers were not able to answer him because they were terrified at his presence. ⁴Then Joseph said to his brothers, "Come close to me." When they had done so, he said, "I am your brother Joseph, the one you sold into Egypt!" ⁵And now, do not be distressed and do not be angry with yourself for selling me here, because I was to save lives that God sent me ahead of you. ⁶For two years now there has been famine in the land, and for the next five years there will not be plowing and reaping. 7But God sent me ahead of you to preserve for you a remnant on earth and to save your lives by great deliverance. ⁸"So then, it was not you who sent me here, but God. He made me father to Pharaoh, lord of his entire household and ruler of all Egypt. ⁹Now hurry back to my father and say to him, "This is what your son Joseph says: God has made me lord of all Egypt. Come down to me; don't delay.

Genesis 37:3, 36; 45: 3-9

AS WE GROW TOGETHER

Week Thirty-Five — Monday
If You Could, Would You Change Your Mind?
Genesis 37: 3-5, 8, 11, 31-36

³Now Israel loved Joseph more than any other sons because he had been born to him in his old age; and he made a richly ornamented robe for him. ⁴When his brothers saw that their father loved him more than any of them, they hated him and could not speak a kind word to him. ⁵ Joseph had a dream, and when he told it to his brothers, they hated him all the more. ⁸His brothers said to him, "Do you intend to reign over us? Will you actually rule us? And they hated him all the more because of his dreams and what he had said. His brothers were jealous of him but his father kept the matter in mind. ³¹Then they got Joseph's robe, slaughtered a goat and dipped the robe in the blood. ³²They took the ornamented robe back to their father and said, "We found this. Examine it to see whether it is your son's robe." ³³He recognized it and said, "It is my son's robe! Some ferocious animal has devoured him. Joseph has surely been torn to pieces." ³⁴Then Jacob tore his clothes, put on sackcloth and mourned for his son many days. ³⁵All his sons and daughters came to comfort him, but he refused to be comforted. "No," he said, "in the morning will I go down to the grave to my son." So his father wept for him. ³⁶Meanwhile, the Midianites sold Joseph in Egypt to Potiphar, one of Pharaoh's officials, the captain of the guard.

Genesis 37: 3-5, 8, 11, 31-36

A Prayer Journal for Expectant Couples

Week Thirty-Five — Tuesday
Jealousy To The Highest Power
Genesis 4: 1-16

¹Adam lay with his wife Eve, and she became pregnant and gave birth to Cain. She said, "With the help of the Lord I have brought forth a man." ²Later she gave birth to his brother Abel. Now Abel kept flocks, and Cain worked the soil. ³In the course of time Cain brought some of he fruits of the soil as an offering to the Lord. ⁴But Abel brought fat portions from some of the firstborn of his flock. The Lord looked with favor on Abel and his offering, ⁵but on Cain and his offering he did not look with favor. So Cain was very angry, and his face was downcast. ⁶Then the Lord said to Cain, "Why are you angry? Why is your face downcast? ⁷If you do what is right will you not be accepted? But if you do not do what is right, sin is crouching at your door; it desires to have you, but you must master it." ⁸Now Cain said to his brother Abel, "Let's go out to the field." And while they were in the field, Cain attacked his brother Abel and killed him. ⁹Then the Lord said to Cain, "Where is your brother Abel?" "I don't know," he replied. "Am I my brothers Keeper?" ¹⁰The Lord said, "hat you have done? Listen! You brother's blood cries out to me from the ground. ¹¹Now you are under a curse and driven from the ground, which opened its mouth to receive your brother's blood from your hand. ¹²When you work the ground, it will no longer yield its crops for you. You will be a restless wanderer on the earth. ¹³Cain said to the Lord, "My punishment is more than I can bear. ¹⁴Today you are driving me from the land, and I will be hidden from your presence, I will be a restless wanderer on the earth, and whoever finds me will kill me." ¹⁵But the Lord said to him, "Not so, if anyone kills Cain, he will suffer vengeance seven times over." Then the Lord put a mark on Cain so that no one who found him would kill him. ¹⁶So Cain went out from the Lord's presence and lived in the land of Nod, east of Eden.

Genesis 4: 1-16

As We Grow Together

Week Thirty-Five — Wednesday
Where You Go, I Will Go
Ruth 1: 16

[16]But Ruth replied, "Don't urge me to leave you or to turn back from you. Where you go I will go, and where you stay I will stay. Your people will be my people and your God my God.

Ruth 1:16

A PRAYER JOURNAL FOR EXPECTANT COUPLES

Week Thirty-Five — Thursday
A Model Father: A True Role Model
Luke 15: 11, 20B, 22-24, 31-32

[11]Jesus continued: "There was a man who had two sons." [20b]But while he was still a long way of, his father saw him and was filled with compassion for him; he ran to his son, threw his arms around him and kissed him. [22]"But the father said to the servants, 'Quick! Bring the best robe and put it on him. Put a ring on his finger and sandals on his feet. [23]Bring the fattened calf and kill it. Let's have a feast and celebrate. [24]For this son of mine was dead and is alive again; he was lost and is found.' So the began to celebrate." [31]"My son,' the father said, 'you are always with me, and everything I have is yours. [32]But we have to celebrate and be glad, because this brother of yours was dead and is alive again; he was lost and is found"

Luke 15: 11, 20B, 22-24, 31-32

As We Grow Together

Week Thirty-Five — Friday
Wisdom Develops Over Time
Luke 15: 12-20a, 21

^{12}The younger said to his father, 'Father, give me my share of the estate.' So he divided his property between them. ^{13}"Not long after that, the younger son got together all he had, set off for a distant country and there squandered his wealth in wild living. ^{14}After he had spent everything, there was a severe famine in that whole country, and he began to be in need. ^{15}So he went and hired himself out to a citizen of that country, who sent him to his fields to feed pigs. ^{16}He longed to fill his stomach with the pods that the pigs were eating, but no one gave him anything. ^{17}When he came to his senses, he said, 'How many of my father's hired men have food to spare, and here I am starving to death! ^{18}I will set out and go back to my father and say to him: Father, I have sinned against heaven and against you. ^{19}I am no longer worthy to be called your son; make me like one of your hired men.' ^{20a}So he got up and went to his father. ^{21}"The son said to him, 'Father, I have sinned against heaven and against you. I am no longer worthy to be called your son.'

Luke 15: 12-20a, 21

A Prayer Journal for Expectant Couples

Week Thirty-Five — Saturday
Can's See the Forest Because of the Trees
Luke 15: 25-30

[25]"Meanwhile, the older son was in the field. When he came near the house, he heard music and dancing. [26]So he called one of his servants and asked him what was going on. [27]'Your brother has come,' he replied. 'and your father has killed the fattened calf because he has him back safe and sound.'" [28]The older became angry and refused to go in. So his father went out and pleaded with him. [29]But he answered his father, 'Look! All these years I've been slaving for you and never disobeyed your orders. Yet you never gave me even a young goat so I could celebrate with my friends. [30]But when this son of yours who has squandered your property with prostitutes comes home, you kill a fattened calf for him!

Luke 15: 25-30

As We Grow Together

Week Thirty-Six
Parenting Great Children
Kids of Great Parents

There are incredible responsibilities for parents. There is a race to educate and train great children. How do these parents do it? As a parent trying to parent great children, we will discuss some great children and the parents of those great children. What are the qualities of the parents and children who are great? How do you groom a President, a leader, a motivator, an anointed one and a history maker? Consider the life and lifestyle of the family who the President of the United States. Consider the life and lifestyle of leaders who create other leaders. Consider the life and lifestyle of families who are not leaders who create leaders.

At first consideration the characteristics includes integrity, honor, honesty, respect, discipline, work ethic, self-control, and leadership. The most important consideration is God is the key factor in each life. Other considerations include motivation, desire, and goal driven.

Quite important is love for your child regardless of what they become. Children spell love: TIME. Try to avoid the myth of purchase power. I substituted in two schools a few years ago and the students were different socio-economically, but they were the same academically. One group didn't drive cars to school. The other group drove Hummers and BMW's and other luxury vehicles to school. The problem is that they want their parent's time rather than the stuff the parents provide.

What kind of time do these "great" parents spend with their parents? What kinds of activities do these families do together? What kind of student do they need to be to be considered "great"? Did they make conscious decisions about avoiding drugs, alcohol, pregnancy, and other distractions as a teen so that they could be great? Do they understand how to avoid events that they will regret later?

As a final note, even when a child or parent does something that may challenge their potential greatness there is still an opportunity to keep the greatness course. Some of my hero's have bad incidents and they still have reached greatness. While the media may not forgive and some family may delay their forgiveness, but God forgives upon request all the time.

Sunday: Jesse: the Father of David
1 Samuel 16: 11

A Prayer Journal for Expectant Couples

Monday: David
              1 Samuel 16: 7, 12-13

Tuesday: Elizabeth and Zechariah
              Luke 1: 5-25

Wednesday: John the Baptist
              Luke 1: 66, 76-80

Thursday: Mary and Joseph
              Luke 1: 26-38

Friday: Jesus
              Luke 2: 42-43, 49-52

Saturday: Paul
              Acts 9

AS WE GROW TOGETHER

Week Thirty-Six — Sunday
Jesse: The Father of David
1 Samuel 16: 11

¹¹So he asked Jesse, "Are these all the sons you have?" "There is still the youngest," Jesse answered, "but he is tending the sheep." Samuel said, "Send for him; we will not sit down until he arrives."

1 Samuel 16: 11

A Prayer Journal for Expectant Couples
Week Thirty-Six — Monday
David
1 Samuel 16: 7, 12-13

[7]"But the Lord said to Samuel, "Do not consider his appearance or his eight for I have rejected him. The Lord does not look at the things man look at. Man looks at the outward appearance, but the Lord looks at the heart." [12b]Then the Lord said, "Rise and anoint him; he is the one."

1 Samuel 16: 7, 12b

As We Grow Together

Week Thirty-Six — Tuesday
Elizabeth and Zechariah
Luke 1: 5-25

[11]Then an angel of the Lord appeared to him, standing at the right side of the altar of incense. [12]When Zechariah saw him, he was startled and was gripped with fear. [13]But the angel said to him: "Do not be afraid, Zechariah; your prayer has been heard. Your wife Elizabeth will bear you a son, and you are to give him the name John. [14]He will be a joy and delight to you, and many will rejoice because if his birth, [15]for he will be great in the sight of the Lord. He is never to take wine or other fermented drink, and he will be filled with the Holy Spirit even from birth. [16]Many if the people of Israel will he bring back to the Lord their God. [17]And he will go on before the Lord, in the spirit and power of Elijah, to turn the hearts of the fathers to their children and the disobedient to the wisdom of the righteous – to make ready a people prepared for the Lord." [18]Zechariah asked the angel, "How can I be sure of this? I am an old man and my wife is well along in years." [19]The angel answered, "I am Gabriel, I stand in the presence of God, and I have been sent to speak to you and to tell you this good news. [20]And now you will come true at their proper time." [21]Meanwhile, the people were waiting for Zechariah and wondering why he stayed so long in the temple. [22]When he came out, he could not speak to them. They realized he had seen a vision in the temple, for he kept making signs to them but remained unable to speak. [23]When his time of service was completed he returned home. [24]After his wife Elizabeth became pregnant and for five months remained in seclusion. [25]"The Lord has done this for me," she said. "In these days he has shown his favor and taken away my disgrace among the people."

Luke 1:11-25

A Prayer Journal for Expectant Couples

Week Thirty-Six — Wednesday
John the Baptist
Luke 1:66, 76-80

[76] And you, my child, will be called a prophet of the Most High; for you will go on before the Lord to prepare the way for Him

Luke 1:76

As We Grow Together

Week Thirty-Six — Thursday
Mary and Joseph
Luke 1:26-38

[37] For nothing is impossible with God.

Luke 1:37

A Prayer Journal for Expectant Couples

Week Thirty-Six — Friday
Jesus
Luke 2:42-43, 49-52

51b But his mother treasured all these things in her heart.

Luke 2:51b

Week Thirty-Six — Saturday
Paul
Acts 9; 13:9

[17]Then Ananias went to the house and entered it. Placing his hands on Saul, he said, "Brother Saul, the Lord—Jesus, who appeared to you on the road as you were coming here—has sent me so that you may see again and be filled with the Holy Spirit."

Acts 9:17

A Prayer Journal for Expectant Couples

Week Thirty-Seven
What Kind of Parent Would Jesus Be?

Jesus Christ was not a parent. Although unfortunate, He was not a parent but would have made a great parent. His character, attitude, and demeanor lends itself well to parenting. He is a also patient and kind and honest. Jesus would make a great parent. Using Him as an example, how can I be a great parent? I personally could use some tweaking of my parenting skills. Parenting gets complicated when issues are added such as financial, or marital or anything that keeps you from focusing on your parenting.

Child abuse is horrible but the actual child abuse takes place with majority women, Caucasian, ages 29-34, and middle class. The majority of the audience of this book fits the description of the average child abuser.

Why does that woman abuse her child? My best guess is based on my volunteer experience, she is overwhelmed with her life and all that her life entails. She doesn't have any help. Family doesn't live close. She and her husband haven't been on a date in months. She doesn't feel good about herself and she is too busy to know it. Take your life, add a child or two, add expenses to a budget that was already stretched, issues with employment, and stir, then you fit the description.

Parenting requires focus on the child. Jesus focused on us individually and collectively. When we are parenting, we have to prioritize what is most important between children and life. The children are the most important, if we forget or get distracted.

Jesus is a profound example of parenting. He knew how to discipline with love and compassion.

Parenting at the level God's prescribes requires love, forgiveness, intercessory, obedience, instruction, spiritual knowledge, and disciplinarian. Parenting also requires compassion, time, attention, research, resourcefulness. God demands your best investment in His children. We are the steward of His children. We need to consider what God has designed for that child and your family. That child carries on your great name. They may make your name great.

Parenting is the key to their success in life. How you treat them is how they expect to be treated in the world. As parents, we have full control of their self-image and self-esteem.

As We Grow Together

Sunday	Loving	John 15:9-14, 17
Monday	Forgiving	Luke 23:34
Tuesday	Intercessor	Matthew 6:9-13; 26-36
Wednesday	Obedient	Mark 14:35-36
Thursday	Teacher	John 7:16-17
Friday	Spiritual	Luke 2:46-47, 49
Saturday	Disciplinarian	Luke 8:24b

A Prayer Journal for Expectant Couples

Week Thirty-Seven — Sunday
Jesus Would be a Loving Parent
John 15:9-14, 17

[9] "As the Father has loved Me, so have I loved you. Now remain in My love. [13] Greater love has no one than this, that he lay down his life for his friends.

John 15:9, 13

AS WE GROW TOGETHER

Week Thirty-Seven — Monday
Jesus Would be a Forgiving Parent
Luke 23:34a; Matthew 18:21-22

[34a]Jesus said, "Father, forgive them for they know not what they are doing."

Luke 23:34a

A Prayer Journal for Expectant Couples

Week Thirty-Seven — Tuesday
Jesus is Our Intercessor as Parent
Matthew 6:9-13; 26:36

[36]Then Jesus went with His disciples to a place called Gethsemane, and he said to them, "Sit here while I go over there and pray."

Matthew 26:36

As We Grow Together

Week Thirty-Seven — Wednesday
Jesus Shows Us Obedience
Mark 14:35-36

[36] "Abba, Father," He said, "Everything is possible for You. Take this cup from Me. Yet not what I will, but what You will."

Mark 14:36

A Prayer Journal for Expectant Couples

Week Thirty-Seven — Thursday
Jesus Is Our Teacher
John 7:16-17

¹⁶Jesus answered, "My teaching is not my own. It comes from Him who sent Me. ¹⁷If anyone chooses to do God's will, He will find out whether My teaching come from God or whether I speak on my own."

John 7:16-17

As We Grow Together

Week Thirty-Seven — Friday
Jesus is Our Spiritual Leader
Luke 2:46-47, 49

⁴⁶After three days they found Him in the temple courts, sitting among the teachers, listening to them and asking them questions. ⁴⁹ "Why were you searching for Me?" He asked. "Didn't you know I had to be in My Father's House?"

Luke 2:46, 49

A Prayer Journal for Expectant Couples
Week Thirty-Seven — Saturday
Jesus As the Disciplinarian Parents
Luke 8:24b

[24b]He got up and rebuked the wind and the raging waters: the storm subsided, and all was calm.

Luke 8:24b

As We Grow Together

Week Thirty-Eight
Parenting Effectively

Jesus effectively influences and assists us to parent. When we consider the sacrifice Jesus made for us to have life. To live on the veil of His mercy, grace, and forgiveness, He shows us how to give those benefits to our children. He teaches us to lead, to offer compassion, to serve, to comfort, to counsel, to provide, and to be faithful as parents.

As a leader and example of what Jesus will do, we had to focus on His actions and His ATTITUDE. As parents, your GREAT attitude makes the difference. Your attitude determines your child's attitude. The cliché of the "apple does not fall far from the tree" holds especially true here. Your response to a situation <u>heavily</u> influences how the child responds to what he/she faces. When I am optimistic and positive, my children respond the same way. When I am not, they respond the same way. In so many ways, I control their response and their behavior with my behavior and responses.

Jesus shows us how to respond and react through how He treated those closest to Him: His disciples. As parents, we have to impart knowledge and wisdom to our children. I know this is the most difficult part of what we do because we have to find time to do it! In our current culture and economy, we have to work two jobs to maintain these "Dream" lifestyles. We work 60-80 hours per week per person to do this maintenance. So this begs the question: "WHO IS WATCHING THE CHILDREN?"

I have a friend who is the mother of three girls and stepmother to two boys. When she quit her job during the third pregnancy, my first thought was 'why would she do that?' But after more consideration, I know that she made the BEST decision. In order for her to work, she took the children to daycare. She was spending her entire paycheck on the daycare, so she was working for someone to watch her children. She decided that spending time with them was more important than working.

I have another friend who responds, "it's not my day to watch them", when she is asked where someone is. When she first said it to me I laughed. One day, I made a choice to pick up my child and return to work with her. It was my day to WATCH her. Spending time with our children is how they learn what we need them to know. It is your turn to spend QUALITY time with your children.

Sunday:	Compassionate as Parent

A Prayer Journal for Expectant Couples

John 11: 35

Monday:	Leader as Parent John 6: 1-2
Tuesday:	Comforter as Parent John 16: 33; Isaiah 66: 13, Matthew 11:28.30
Wednesday:	Servant as Parent John 13: 5-17
Thursday:	Faithful as Parent Hebrews 11: 6
Friday:	Counselor as Parent Isaiah 9: 6
Saturday:	Provider as Parent John 6: 11-13

AS WE GROW TOGETHER

Week Thirty-Eight — Sunday
Compassionate as Parent
John 11:35

[35] Jesus wept.

John 11:35

A Prayer Journal for Expectant Couples
Week Thirty-Eight — Monday
Leader as Parent
John 6: 2

²and a great crowd of people followed Him because they saw the miraculous signs he had performed in the sick.

John 6: 2

As We Grow Together
Week Thirty-Eight — Tuesday
Comforter as Parent
John 16:33; Isaiah 66:13; Matthew 11:28, 30

^{33}"I have told you these things, so that in me you may have peace. In this world you will have trouble. But take heart! I have overcome the world"

^{13}As a mother comforts her child, so will I comfort you; and you will be comforted over Jerusalem."

^{28}"Come to me. All you who are weary and burdened, and I will give you rest. ^{30} For my yoke is easy and my burden is light.

John 16:33; Isaiah 66:13; Matthew 11:28, 30

A Prayer Journal for Expectant Couples

Week Thirty-Eight — Wednesday
Servant as Parent
John 13: 16

¹⁶ I tell you the truth, no servant is greater than his master, nor is a messenger greater than the one who sent him.

John 13: 16

AS WE GROW TOGETHER

Week Thirty-Eight — Thursday
Faithful as Parent
Hebrews 11: 6

⁶ And without faith it is impossible to please God, because anyone who comes to Him must believe that He exists and that He rewards those who earnestly seek Him.

Hebrews 11: 6

A Prayer Journal for Expectant Couples
Week Thirty-Eight — Friday
Counselor as Parent
Isaiah 9: 6

⁶ For to us a child is born, to us a Son is given, and the government will be on His shoulders. And He will be called Wonderful Counselor, Mighty God, Everlasting Father, Prince of Peace.

Isaiah 9: 6

AS WE GROW TOGETHER

Week Thirty-Eight — Saturday
Provider as Parent
John 6: 11-13

[11] Jesus then took the loaves, gave thanks, and distributed to those who were seated as much as they wanted. He did the same with the fish. [12] When they had all had enough to eat, he said to the disciples, "Gather the pieces that are left over. Let nothing be wasted." [13] So they gathered them and filled twelve baskets with the pieces of the five barley loaves left by those who had eaten.

John 6: 11-13

A PRAYER JOURNAL FOR EXPECTANT COUPLES

Week Thirty-Nine
Relax

Around the time the baby is about to arrive, we start nesting meaning we clean and straighten and organize and fluff. We have this energy burst and become excited and we need to RELAX! We need to sit down and RELAX! After the baby arrives, RELAX will be a distant memory. Relax is defined however you decide. Relax for me is a manicure or pedicure or a nap or a message or a long drive or just QUIET.

As a mother, I have to schedule the Relax. I have to take my babies to the salon with me so I could get these things done. Those trips were far from relaxing. You may have to be creative about how this happens after the baby arrives, so do all you can now.

Encourage your spouse to Relax as well. Life changes completely when the baby is born. I have a cousin who told my husband when we married that he could kiss his golf good-bye. My husband didn't believe her. He knows better now. His time to play golf has severely diminished and the resources too.

Relax! Kick your feet up. Listen to all the songs on your iPod or MP3 player. Take time for yourself. Savor the nuances that you have personally taken for granted. Cherish waking up on your schedule rather than the schedule of a little one. Close your eyes and enjoy the silence. Stop scheduling things that don't involve RELAX!

Go sit with your friends, family and associates, which you have been promising all this time. Keep the moments fresh. Relax. Spend time with your spouse doing the things that you did when you met and dated. Read all of your magazines that you usually just skim, or never read at all.

Relax facilitates the refuel, the re-energizing and re-evaluate. If you appreciate the RELAX now, when you need to relax, it won't be foreign. Likewise, your appreciation will be great making the RELAX that valuable. When you are able to RELAX, you don't usually get overwhelmed. As a parent, you will face some difficult times. Knowing how to relax is critical for keeping a balanced household and life.

RELAX!

Sunday: Enjoy each other
Song of Solomon

AS WE GROW TOGETHER

Monday: Enjoy Hot Meals

Tuesday: Enjoy Warm Baths

Wednesday: Enjoy Quiet Time

Thursday: Enjoy Other People

Friday: Enjoy a Clean House

Saturday: Enjoy sleep

A Prayer Journal for Expectant Couples

Week Thirty-Nine — Sunday
Enjoy Each Other

As a married couple, you have been intimate during cooking, quiet time, and bed time, just to name a few. The fact is that your creativity is about to be exercised – fully and completely. Enjoy this time together before the baby arrives. Talk to each other as often as possible. Talking as a couple changes as soon as the child starts talking.

As We Grow Together

Week Thirty-Nine — Monday
Enjoy Hot Meals

A couple stopped at my table and encouraged me to enjoy my hot meals. I laughed until they left, but realized that I hadn't thought of that. They were correct by the way.

ENJOY HOT MEALS! ENJOY ALL MEALS!

A Prayer Journal for Expectant Couples
Week Thirty-Nine — Tuesday
Enjoy Warm Baths

When my day was difficult when I was single, I would come home and take a long hot bath. When I would take that longer than normal bath, I could take my time and use all those products I purchase from Bath & Body Works. With a new baby, the long bath time does not happen as often, but the days are not easier. Now the long baths are further and further apart. We talked about the RELAX. The bath is one of my techniques. With the bath at risk, I have to deal with replacing the bath with something else. It is a process to establish a stress relieving mechanism. It is important to do this. Parenting can be overwhelming. That stress relief helps pass the overwhelming parts of parenting.

As We Grow Together

Week Thirty-Nine — Wednesday
Enjoy Quiet Time

I love to sleep. I love to sleep-in. I love to sleep late. I love to take naps. I like to read. I like to write. I like to listen to music. None of these "likes" includes talking.

A Prayer Journal for Expectant Couples
Week Thirty-Nine — Thursday
Enjoy Other People

Giving up relationships when you get married and losing more when you have children is a BIG MISTAKE!

Iron sharpens iron! Keep yourself around people that will lift you, rather than bring you down, feed you with positive feedback and information, support your ideas no matter what happens and who you enjoy.

As We Grow Together

Week Thirty-Nine — Friday
Enjoy a Clean House

Your home may be showroom clean and detailed. Mine once was. I decided that once my home was out of hand, I left it there. I do not have any help. My children are learning to clean up after themselves. So when they are older, my home will return to showcase status.

A Prayer Journal for Expectant Couples
Week Thirty-Nine — Saturday
Enjoy Sleep!

SLEEP! I would love to sleep late on Saturday mornings. I define late as wake up on my own, rather than being awakened by a cry or a pat or a voice. This may never happen again, however I do try.

Week Forty
Seven Days of Prayer

Start your seven days of prayer. Prayer summons power. God hears us when we pray. Seven days of prayer will fill you with His presence and guidance and instruction.

We have discussed completely that prayer is the communication that we need to be within God's will. Prayer is designed to face the issues we address as parents. Prayer is REQUIRED! Seven days of prayer influences your life, your marriage, your child(ren), and your circumstances.

Seven days of prayer can include your entire family or your extended family. Set a special time for prayer. At that agreed upon time, raise the prayer concerns. Pray for as long as God leads you and speaks to you.

From the days of prayer, you will access the power you need to keep focused on your child. The power of prayer keeps us from being overwhelmed. Pray as a couple. PRAY as a couple! Pray as a COUPLE! PRAY AS A COUPLE!

God has gifted you as a couple to be a couple, to have a child together, and have given you the stewardship of that child. You need to access God for your needs. He is waiting for you to ask in Jesus' name for what you need and your heart desires.

Pray for all things that you are thinking about and what you need and whatever overwhelms you and what scares you and what hurts you and what excites you. Pay about everything. I Thessalonians 5: 12 states, "Pray continually." All the time! Yes, when you break the tape closure for the diaper, PRAY! Nothing is too silly or too small for God.

Prayer accesses POWER! Prayer lifts your head! Prayer reintroduces the positive. Prayer reminds us that we are not alone.

Pray together. Fast together. Feel together. Prayer reminds us not to internalize, rather to verbalize to God and to each other what is happening. The communication is critical to maintaining healthy relationships.

You will need this POWER. PRAYER stimulates POWER. PRAYER summons POWER from above and within. God ANSWERS PRAYER!

Sunday: Pray for Health

A Prayer Journal for Expectant Couples

Tuesday: Pray for Cohesion in Your Marriage

Wednesday: Pray for Guidance as a Parent

Thursday: Pray for Trust, Faith, and Confidence

Friday: Pray for God's Favor

Saturday: Pray for God's Peace

As We Grow Together

Week Forty — Sunday
Pray for Health

Your health is important. Your child's health is important. You get one body. You are the steward of that body. This means that we have to be conscious of what we eat, how we live and how we exercise or NOT. Get to know your family's health history. TAKE THIS SERIOUSLY. I have history of diabetes in my family. I am careful about how I eat. I have to exercise. I maintain my weight. I get regular check-ups and blood work so that I know where I am. I do not want diabetes. I do not want that lifestyle. I lived through that as a child.

_____
_____
_____
_____
_____
_____
_____
_____
_____
_____
_____
_____
_____
_____
_____
_____
_____
_____
_____
_____
_____
_____
_____

A Prayer Journal for Expectant Couples

Week Forty — Monday
Pray for Cohesion (New or Renewed) in Your Marriage

Marriage is HARD. Adding children to your marriage increases the difficulty level of the marriage. Children demand you divide your time, responsibilities, and finances. These demands can cause strained cohesion in your marriage.

As We Grow Together

Week Forty — Tuesday
Pray for Guidance as a Parent

Parenting is a difficult job, at best. Why we sign up for and ask to be here, I will always question. Children are gifts from God. He plants them where He plans to do His best work. Children change your life – all aspects. As adults, our adjustment time is slow. Where we need immediate transition, we are still on gradual changes.

A Prayer Journal for Expectant Couples

Week Forty — Wednesday
Pray for the Release if Fear, Anxiety and Doubt

Parenting can be scary. You are the steward of that child's life. You can do this. God is there with you through your parenting. Yes, there are things to fear about parenting. How do I feed this child? How do I care for this child? Who is going to care for my child while I a working? What happens if they fall and bleed? Who will be the pediatrician? What is a pediatrician? God gifted you with this child so He has prepared you and sent someone to help you. He may have sent others as well to help you.

Pray.

As We Grow Together

Week Forty — Thursday
Pray for Trust, Faith, and Confidence

Parenting is a TEST of your trust, faith, and confidence. Trust is dedication to God – not your mate, not your family or friends or others, and not yourself. TRUST is limited to and focused on God, Jesus Christ and the Holy Spirit.

Pray.

A Prayer Journal for Expectant Couples

Week Forty — Friday
Pray for God's Favor
"All Things Work Together"

We are on the sixth day of prayer for today. We are asking for God's favor. We are asking for God's favor with full faith and confidence that God will deliver.

As We Grow Together

Week Forty — Saturday
Pray for God's Peace
"Which Transcends All Understanding"

"Jesus loves me this I know for the Bible tells me so. Little ones to Him belong they are weak but He is strong. Yes, Jesus loves me. Yes, Jesus loves me. Yes, Jesus loves me for the Bible tells me so." I sing this song to all babies. I started with mine.

Afterword

Dear Parent:

As We Grow Together has three important connotations: (1) as we grow together closer to Christ personally, (2) as we grow closer together as mother and child and as the father develops a bond with the child, and, (3) as we grow closer together as a couple.

It is my sincere prayer that this has blessed your relationships with God, Jesus and the Holy Spirit, as well as your mate, your child(ren) and family. Growth is all about relationships. When we enhance our relationships, we elevate others above ourselves.

Please let the Holy Spirit be your guide as you make decisions for your child. There are decisions that are not permanent, so that a mistake does not have long term effects. On the other hand, long term effects of decision require study and prayer and wise counsel.

It is my prayer that we have established some foundational Biblical principles that will be accessed as you and your child grow. I know this does not cover every issue that you will ever encounter, however, you have new tools which you can use to be an effective, Christian parent.

Congratulations on this journey. Be careful to not miss anything that could be considered special. Also keep in mind you establish the pace and routine your children experience.

In His name and because of His love,

Onedia N. Gage

Acknowledgements

God, thank You for Your plans for me. Thank You for *As We Grow Together* and choosing me to complete Your project. I just want to please You. Thank You for continuing to anoint me and to invest in me and my gifts, which keep surprising me. Thank You for loving and forgiving me.

Family, thank you for supporting me and my endeavors. Thank you for loving me, especially when I do nothing without a pen and a clipboard. Hillary and Nehemiah, thank you for enduring my late nights, your ideas, the sounding board, the love and the support.

To my editor, Tassandra Allen. Thanks for the feedback and the discussions. The bantering has grown me and my writing. Thanks for enforcing the standard. Thank you for raising the bar of standards.

To my graphic artist, Ron Nicholson and Picture Perfect Designs. Thanks for the art and imagination, for making my words look fabulous.

To my prayer partners and to my accountability partners, thank you for the long talks and the powerful prayers and the encouragement.

To Mrs. Iris Jackson, thank you for typing such an overwhelming project.

To you, may these words impact your parenting and divulge the secrets of parenting others have chosen to keep to themselves.

A PRAYER JOURNAL FOR EXPECTANT COUPLES

Minister Onedia N. Gage seeks to share her outlandish pursuit of God with her prayers, study and meditation. She desires to share her faith in a manner which helps you do the same through her calling. She hopes that these words bless you.
Please feel free to contact and share your testimony.
onediagage@onediagage.com, or @onediangage (twitter).
www.onediagage.com
Blogtalkradio.com/onediagage
Youtube.com/onediagage
Facebook.com/onedia-gage-ministries

A Prayer Journal for Expectant Couples

AS WE GROW TOGETHER
PREACHER ♦ ADVOCATE ♦ TEACHER ♦ FACILITATOR
CONFERENCE SPEAKER ♦ WORKSHOP LEADER

To invite Rev. Gage to speak at your church, women's ministry,
Or any other ministry.

Please contact us at: www.onedigage.com
@onediangage (twitter) ♦ onediagage@onediagage.com ♦
facebook.com/onediagageministries
youtube.com/onediagage ♦ blogtalkradio.com/onediagage ♦
ongage (Instagram)

A Prayer Journal for Expectant Couples

AS WE GROW TOGETHER

Publishing

Do you have a book you want to write, but do not know what to do?

Do you have a book you need to publish but do not know how to start?

Would publishing move your career forward?

Let us help

onediagage@purpleink.net ♦ www.purpleink.net

281.740.5143 ♦ 512.715.4243

www.ingramcontent.com/pod-product-compliance
Lightning Source LLC
Chambersburg PA
CBHW022047160426
43198CB00008B/147